# A. E. WAITE: SELECTED MASONIC PAPERS

*Also in this series*

**THE BOOK OF THE LODGE**
George Oliver
*Introduction by Richard Sandbach*

**ILLUSTRATIONS OF MASONRY**
William Preston
*Introduction by Colin Dyer*

**KING SOLOMON'S TEMPLE IN THE MASONIC TRADITION**
Alexander Horne
*Introduction by Harry Carr*

**MASONIC FACTS AND FICTIONS**
Henry Sadler
*Introduction by John Hamill*

**THE ROYAL MASONIC CYCLOPAEDIA**
Kenneth Mackenzie
*Introduction by John Hamill and R. A. Gilbert*

**THE SPIRIT OF MASONRY**
William Hutchinson
*Introduction by Trevor Stewart*

# A. E. WAITE: SELECTED MASONIC PAPERS

Edited and Introduced by
Edward Dunning

THE AQUARIAN PRESS

First published 1988

© THE AQUARIAN PRESS 1988

*All rights reserved. No part of this book may be reproduced or utilized in any form or by any means, electronic or mechanical, including photocopying, recording or by any information storage and retrieval system, without permission in writing from the Publisher.*

British Library Cataloguing in Publication Data

Waite, Arthur Edward
Selected masonic papers.—(Masonic classics series)
1. Hermetism
I. Title   II. Dunning, Edward
III. Series
299'.93     BL820.M5

ISBN 0-85030-613-2

*The Aquarian Press is part of the Thorsons Publishing Group, Wellingborough, Northamptonshire, NN8 2RQ, England*

Printed in Great Britain by Woolnough Bookbinding Limited, Irthlingborough, Northamptonshire

2  4  6  8  10  9  7  5  3  1

# CONTENTS

*Introduction*   9

*Chapter*
1. Discourse on the Fellowcraft Degree   13
2. Masonic Tradition and the Royal Arch   19
3. Robert Fludd and Freemasonry   31
4. Hermetic Schools and Masonry   45
5. The Royal and Masonic Art   73
6. A Lodge of Magic   87
7. The Templar Orders in Freemasonry   97
8. The Grade of Kadosh   117
9. The Spiritual Symbolism of Freemasonry   123
10. Some Deeper Aspects of Masonic Symbolism   153
11. The Veil of the Sanctum Sanctorum   171

*Index of Proper Names*   187

# MASONIC CLASSICS SERIES

Freemasonry has an extensive literature but much of it, having been written for a specialized readership and published in short runs, is now out of print. This series has been designed to provide both the serious student and the general reader with an opportunity of reading a wide cross section of classic works of Freemasonry. It is proposed to include standard historical works which have influenced the historiography of Freemasonry by authors such as Sadler, Hughan, Oliver, and Gould; texts basic to an understanding of Freemasonry, such as the Old Charges and Constitutions; contemporary handbooks and commentaries produced to explain Freemasonry to its members, such as the works of Preston, Hutchinson, and Calcott; and Masonic oddities such as Mackenzie's idiosyncratic *Royal Masonic Cyclopaedia*.

Each volume will consist of a facsimile of the original text, or the best edition if more than one was published, prefaced by a critical introduction by an acknowledged authority on the subject. The introduction will describe the author of the text and place his work in the context of its time and its relevance to the development of Freemasonry or its historiography.

JOHN HAMILL
*Series Editor*

# INTRODUCTION

THE apologists of Freemasonry have been many and varied, uniting only to defend the Craft from the periodic attacks made upon it—although some of their defences, it may be said, have done more harm than the original attacks—and more often arguing vociferously over just what it is that they are so vigorously defending, and whence it came.

Freemasonry defines itself, in the English Constitution at least, as 'a peculiar system of Morality, veiled in Allegory, and illustrated by Symbols', and the book of *Constitutions* lays down clear rules for regulating the workings of Craft lodges—but beyond this it does not go, for just as the United Grand Lodge of England makes no official pronouncements on theological dogma (for Freemasonry is not, in any sense, a religion), so it subscribes to no particular theory of the origin of the Craft.

Individual freemasons, however, are free to believe what they wish about the origin, meaning, and purpose of Freemasonry, and this freedom has been exercised to the full. Before the development, during the later nineteenth century, of what is termed the 'authentic' school of masonic research—in which indisputable documentary evidence is the basis of all theory—it was commonplace for masonic writers to claim a vast antiquity for Freemasonry, and to place its origin among the Hebrew patriarchs.

Nineteenth-century occultists, many of whom were freemasons, took up these dubious ideas and grafted them on to their own eccentric speculations about the nature of Freemasonry, which they—as followers of the 'esoteric' rather than the 'authentic' school of research—saw as an integral part of the

Western Mystery Tradition, and a direct descendant of the Mystery Schools of antiquity. They failed, however, to produce the slightest objective evidence that Freemasonry as we know it is derived from such sources, or that its ceremonies have any connection, other than the possession of those general features common to all initiatory rites, with Egyptian, Eleusinian, Mithraic or any other esoteric set of rituals.

As a consequence of this misdirected enthusiasm, more recent masonic scholarship has rejected as invalid any approach to the problem of masonic history which does not conform to the canons of the 'authentic' school, and in so doing has made itself the poorer by denying a hearing to those scholars who have adopted a non-authentic approach but who remain gifted and original thinkers. It is, for example, quite unjust to equate an historian as unreliable and 'inventive' (to use a kind expression) as John Yarker, with an inspired mystic of such undoubted integrity as W. L. Wilmshurst and to condemn them as equally unworthy.

Yet it must be admitted that it is no easy task to find a masonic scholar who at the same time recognized the need for careful and accurate documentation and also brought the insights of a mystic to the problems of masonic history and symbols. Perhaps only one man was so qualified: the scholar and mystic, A. E. Waite.

Waite, however, was no mere codifier of historical data. For him Freemasonry was something more than 'a peculiar system of Morality'—he saw it as part of that Secret Tradition which is 'the immemorial knowledge concerning man's way of return whence he came by a method of the inward life' (*Secret Tradition in Freemasonry*, Vol. 2, p.379). Every aspect of that tradition, whether in alchemy, kabalism, Rosicrucianism or Freemasonry itself, was a means to an end, a 'Way of Divine Union' that would lead man back to both an understanding and a direct experience of God. But although present in all esoteric traditions, the Way remains hidden: 'the keepers of the tradition', said Waite, 'perpetuated it in secret by means of Instituted Mysteries and cryptic literature' (*op. cit.*, Vol. 1, p.*ix*).

In Freemasonry it is revealed by a proper understanding of the rituals, all of which, to qualify as truly masonic, must include symbolic elements of loss and restoration, as well as a third element: 'The middle term is absence, out of which quest arises.

When one of the triad is wanting, whether implicitly or explicitly, the Grade is not Masonic' (*op. cit.* Vol. 2, p.379). Nor was this all, for Waite's concept of saving knowledge was not Gnosticism, but a knowledge of Christ, and Freemasonry was thus—for him—Christian in both origin and essence. He made this clear in his comments on the Royal Arch and the Mark degrees: 'As the Mark restored to Masonry the lost notion of Christhood, so did the Royal Arch bring it back to Trinitarian Doctrine, the Father, the Word and the Spirit, as the Mystical Lecture specifies, described as "the climax of Freemasonry" (*Shadows of Life and Thought*, p.178).

This is not a view shared, certainly not in Waite's sense of it, by the majority of masonic scholars, who have, perhaps, been prejudiced against his historical studies (which were admittedly restricted by his lack of access to many continental archives) as much because of his beliefs as from any flaws in his arguments. And those beliefs, as they appeared to the outside world, were presumed to reflect his personal enthusiasms—all of which appeared to fall within the bounds of occultism and to have been well established before Waite became a freemason.

Waite himself always rejected the label of occultist. He was, he said, 'the exponent in poetical and prose writings of sacramental religion and the higher mysticism, understood in its absolute separation from psychic and occult phenomena', a world-view undoubtedly shaped in large part by the course of his life. He was born in Brooklyn, New York, in 1857, was brought to England as an infant by his widowed mother and raised in near poverty in the suburbs of London. He was also raised as a Roman Catholic, and the influence of the Latin Mass remained with him throughout his life, although he turned from the Church to Spiritualism—and thence to Theosophy and the kabalah—after the death of his sister in 1874.

After ten years studying the traditions of occultism, Waite began to write about them, his earliest works in this field being translations from Eliphas Lévi and his *Real History of the Rosicrucians*. These were rapidly followed by *The Occult Sciences* (1891), his long series of alchemical translations and editions, and his first truly mystical work, *Azoth: The Star in the East* (1893). He also wrote, but did not publish, *The Esoteric History of Freemasonry*, a remarkable work that was completed almost ten years before his initiation into Freemasonry. He was already familiar with the practical side of occultism, having joined the Hermetic Order of the Golden Dawn in 1891, and it was through the influence of one of his colleagues in the Order, Ralph Palmer Thomas, that he finally entered the Craft.

Waite was initiated in Runymede Lodge No. 2430, at Wraysbury on 19 September 1901, raised in the following February, and exalted in Metropolitan Chapter No. 1507 of the Holy Royal Arch in May 1902. But it was the Higher Grades that called him. He was advanced in the Mark Degree in 1905, installed as a Knight Templar in 1902, Perfected in the Ancient and Accepted Rite in 1909, and joined many of the smaller and more obscure Orders, both masonic and quasi-masonic. Parallel to these activities was his work in the Golden Dawn, a branch of which came under his control in 1903, to be reconstituted in 1915 as the Fellowship of the Rosy Cross. Here he guided the members towards a practical realization of the Secret Tradition expounded through the rituals he developed.

This, of course, he could not do within orthodox Freemasonry and his ideas were presented instead by way of the books he wrote: *The Secret Tradition in Freemasonry* (1911, revised ed. 1937), *A New Encyclopaedia of Freemasonry* (1921), and *Emblematic Freemasonry* (1925). His earlier work was well-received, but the *New Encyclopaedia* was castigated, with some justice, for its odd arrangement and its many errors of fact. It remains, however, the only convenient source for details of many obscure areas of masonic history. Waite also lectured extensively and many of his lectures and addresses were printed in masonic or esoteric periodicals, but few of these had any wide distribution, and after his death in 1942 they were largely forgotten.

It is from these unknown and forgotten papers that the present selection has been made—for the benefit of those unbiased readers of his work who, while demanding historical reliability, are principally seekers after spiritual truth and who will draw much from Waite that is denied to entrenched scholars. The true student will seek the meaning behind the form, the message within the words—and in the writings of A. E. Waite he will find, if he looks, both that meaning and that message.

EDWARD DUNNING
*Hampstead, London, December 1986*

# I
# DISCOURSE ON THE FELLOWCRAFT DEGREE

With the exception of a certain number of historical, biographical and descriptive entries in his *New Encyclopaedia of Freemasonry*, Waite wrote almost nothing that was specifically concerned with the Craft Degrees as opposed to those Degrees that lie 'beyond the Craft'. It yet seems appropriate that this selection of his studies of masonic symbolism and tradition should be prefaced by one of his few essays on Craft Masonry—for every mason who aspires to the 'High Grades' must first pass through the three degrees of Entered Apprentice, Fellowcraft, and Master Mason. Waite's *Discourse* was printed in an American masonic journal, *The Builder* (which was edited by his friend, Joseph Fort Newton), in 1917, but was evidently first delivered as an address in a Craft Lodge, although when and in which Lodge is not known.

BRETHREN of the Order, and those among you in particular who have been received recently among us, there is no period too early to conceive a just and commensurate notion of the great institution to which we belong, and in which we have been incorporated as a part of its living body. It is desirable, in the first place, that we should understand certain intimations which occur in the Grade of Neophyte and in that of Fellow Craft. They are open on their surface to misconstruction, and did we afterwards pursue our researches into the history of Emblematic Freemasonry, it might even be thought that they were untrue unless we carried them further than is done commonly. Moreover, in the absence of such researches, they might come to be regarded as so many figures of speech.

The Entered Apprentice is told at an early stage of his experience that the Order possesses great and inestimable privileges as well as those secrets and mysteries concerning which he is sworn to inviolable secrecy. You will observe that the privileges are enumerated separately from the secrets, though the latter stand also for privileges. Among these I will particularize the Signs and Words of the successive Degrees. The privileges imparted by these include the right of entrance to a Lodge, as a guest or subscribing member. They are the titles of our initiation and assuredly they are more than valuable after their own kind, but they do not respond in themselves to the very wide claim which I have mentioned. I conceive therefore that there are other privileges. These are not, however, to be identified with the things implied by the great principles of the Order, precious as are the latter to our hearts, and advantageous as it must ever be to dwell within a circle of fellowship which recognizes the principles of solidarity and will at need extend them in good will to us. They are not in the category of those things which we seek to reserve to worthy men alone. They are rather the marks, seals and characters which it is our sacred duty to display and by which Masonry is known all over the world in its practice of beneficence, benevolence and fraternity, by the love of moral truth and by the truth which abides in honour. I conclude, therefore, that the reference to inestimable privileges is itself in the nature of a mystery and covers things which do not exactly appear on the literal side of our rituals. This is the first point which I am now seeking to commemorate.

The second is concerned more especially with the obligation of the Neophyte Grade in which the Candidate is pledged to hele, conceal and never reveal the secret art and hidden mysteries of Masonry. I believe that after a little reflection I shall carry with me the concurring voice of every Brother amongst us, if I say that this pledge, with the penalties attached thereto, must cover more than the simple signs, tokens, words and procedure which takes place in our Lodges, or too elaborate machinery may be thought to be put in motion than the end appears to require. Hence again it seems certain that the reference to secret arts and hidden mysteries is itself in the nature of a mystery and covers things which do not precisely appear on the literal surface of our Rituals. This is the next point which I am seeking to commemorate here.

For the third, we must pass from the Grade of Initiate or Neophyte to that of Fellow Craft in which there is a brief but singularly pregnant account (1) of that which was attained by the Candidate when he was made an Entered Apprentice; and (2) of that which he is expected to perform in his new capacity as a Craftsman. In the one it is pointed out that he has made himself acquainted with the principles of moral truth and virtue. Now, this is literally true, subject to a single reserve: as one newly admitted, he was not intended to be tried beyond his strength: the principles which he is said to have acquired were in reality communicated to him without action on his own part, but he was left in the First Degree to reflect upon them. They are actually the root matter and sum total of moral truth and all natural virtue. It is otherwise in the Degree of Fellow Craft. There it is assumed that the Masonic horizon has opened before and about him, and that he is prepared to enter an almost immeasurable region. He is accordingly advised (1) that he is expected to make the liberal arts and sciences his future study, and (2) that he is permitted to extend his researches into the hidden mysteries of Nature and science. Once again, this is an intimation which covers much more than appears on the literal surface and is a mystery which is expressed shortly but not explained in our Rituals. Here is the third point which I am now seeking to commemorate.

Let us see if there is any direction in which we can turn for a little light on these problems, and as it so happens we shall not have to go outside the Lodge itself.

On his first entrance into Freemasonry the newly received Brother will perceive that he has come into a world of emblems or symbolism, and that whatsoever takes place therein has a meaning behind it which is by no means indicated invariably on the surface. Sometimes, and indeed frequently, there is more than one inward meaning, depending on the point of view from which it is approached. The Lodge is an eloquent example of this truth. When its door opens for the Candidate he enters into an institution which has its branches spread over the four quarters of the globe. It may be a very small Lodge: it may be a Lodge of poor Brothers only: but whosoever is received therein is recognized through the Masonic world, in all countries and among all peoples. But there is more even than this: however humble in its appointments and proportions, that Lodge is a Microcosm, a symbol, a speaking likeness of universal Freemasonry. It represents also and contains the life of Masonry, and the Ceremony of his initiation integrates the new-made Brother in that peculiar quality of life which is the principle and essence of the Order. He becomes part of an organic whole. In the third place, the Lodge is held to represent the three dimensions of space—that is to say, the universe itself as a cosmos: in length from East to West, in breadth between North and South, in depth from the surface to the centre, and even as high as the heavens.

It is therefore as if the Candidate on his initiation had been born anew into the universe, or that a door had opened to admit him into another cosmos. He comes with his eyes dim and with a restraint about him; he is kept for a considerable period in a state of darkness and bondage: ultimately he is instructed, and that which he finds about him is truly the symbolic representation of a new world. For him at that moment all things seem to be renewed, and it is very soon after this strange and wonderful experience that he is given a key to the meaning. He is told that he is the corner stone of a new foundation, from which he has to build up himself after another and higher manner. In other words, he has to remake his inward nature according to the perfection of the standard which is prescribed by Masonry. It is a moral standard in respect of his dealings with his Brethren and with mankind at large. It is a spiritual standard in respect of his duty towards God, and through obedience thereto it is hoped, held and known that he will ascend to the home of the spirit in the heavenly kingdom, by means of the ladder of Jacob, the successive rounds of which are called by many names, but chief among these are faith, hope and charity. It follows that he has a two-fold work to perform, but it is all in the training of himself. If he be successful, the result will be perfect in its parts and honourable to the builder. From this point of view, the just, perfect and regular Lodge is also a symbol of the man in that state which he is called to attain.

Now, the word initiate, with which we are so familiar in Masonry, signifies a person who has made a new beginning, who has entered a path of experience heretofore untravelled. Its equivalent in other orders and fraternities is the word Neophyte. The Neophyte is also one who has made a new beginning and the term, which is Greek in its origin, signifies him who is reborn, a new plant, one who is remade. In the old instituted mysteries, like those of Samothrace, of Egypt and of Eleusis, the

Candidate was regenerated or reborn—he was otherwise transferred or grafted—at the beginning of his experience, and afterwards he passed through successive stages of a new life till he attained the culminating Grade. It was the same experiment as that of Craft Masonry, in which the Candidate—as an Entered Apprentice—lays the foundation stone of that new building himself, raises a superstructure according to the law and order that Masonry has imposed upon him, continues the erection as a Craftsman, in which Degree the mysteries of Nature and science, recommended to his study, are mysteries of God and the estimation of His wonderful works till at last he puts on the capstone when the Lodge is open in the Sublime Grade of Master.

Our secret art is therefore an art of life, an art of perfection, an art of creation according to a prescribed standard recognized in Masonry: our hidden mysteries are those of our own relations to God, man and the universe, that we may be enabled to fulfill by Masonry the higher law of our being. The inestimable privileges of Masonry include those of its symbolism, the study of which is for our instruction in this high mode of self-building. The arts and mysteries which we are pledged to conceal from the profane are also those of the peculiar law of life in Masonry by which these ends can be reached. Those who are outside the Lodge must come within it, if they desire to share in that life. It is really incommunicable beyond the mystic circle, for the simple reason that it is life itself and not one of its substitutes. While therefore we are properly pledged concerning it, there is something which we could not impart if we tried. In some of the old mysteries, from which we are indirectly descended, initiation and its sequels meant real instruction in this subject, and several of our most suggestive intimations are reflections from that remote source.

And seeing that the Grade of Master Mason is not so much a reflection as the very root, essence and quintessence, of those mysteries, and may be shortly described as an experiment in the deep mystery by which the soul passes through mortal life towards that life in God which is the end of all the mysteries, it comes about in this manner, my Brethren, that we are incorporated with all the great orders and sodalities of the far past and are therefore justified when we say that the meaning of our Masonic Badge is more ancient than the Golden Fleece and that our honourable institution—though under many transformations—has subsisted from time immemorial.

# 2
# MASONIC TRADITION AND THE ROYAL ARCH

The Holy Royal Arch, which is properly understood not as an additional 'degree' but as the completion of the degree of Master Mason in Craft Masonry, was seen by Waite as 'the Grade of the Word attained' and interpreted by him in Trinitarian Christian terms, although it is not today, and was not in Waite's time, a specifically Christian ritual. For Waite it was a gate through which the mystically inclined freemason could enter upon that Way of Divine Union which he saw as the very essence of the Secret Tradition in Freemasonry. His paper on *Masonic Tradition and the Royal Arch* was rewritten in 1925 for inclusion in his book *Emblematic Freemasonry*, where it appears as Chapter V—but in that altered form it would lose its essential meaning if printed independently of the whole work, and so the text that follows is that of the version read to the Somerset Masters' Lodge No. 3746 at Bath, in February 1921, and printed in their *Transactions* for that year.

THE old distinction between Blue and Red has almost fallen into desuetude, so far as normal parlance is concerned, among members of the Craft in England; but we know that a memorial remains among us in the colour-symbolism found in the ROYAL ARCH. The Blue also connotes Symbolical Masonry, and this is a valid qualification, because the Third Degree opens a door into a great figurative Mystery as into the blue distance. It is not of our concern now or we might dwell for a moment on the significant fact that in Irish Craft workings the Candidate is told invariably that even the official and conventional penalties of the Three Degrees are to be regarded as a part integral of the symbolism which rules in all. The ROYAL ARCH, or Red Masonry, has passed by its hypothesis out the symbolical domain: on the surface, at least, it is dealing no longer with allegory, but with an actual historical event. According to that version of the Holy Order which is at work in England and Wales, under the obedience of the Supreme Grand Chapter, it belongs—as we are all well aware—to the time of Zerubbabel and the building of the Second Temple. With certain variations, which are not essential in character, it is the same, I believe, in Scotland and the United States. In Ireland the historical time of the Grade is much later, being that of Josiah the King, but of this I am unable to speak except by report, as there are no Rituals available. There is a sense, however, in which all differences draw to the same end, for all are concerned with the central fact of a Secret Tradition, perpetuated by its hypothesis from an immemorial past, derived originally from sources behind Masonry and carried from Degrees leading up to the ROYAL ARCH, through the Holy Order itself and thence into Christian and some other High Grades.

It is a remarkable fact that on the surface of the Craft Degrees there is practically no intimation of this traditional inheritance. The presumable explanation is that those who constructed the Legend of the Third Degree, following any vestiges which may have come into hands of the 18th Century from the part of York or Scotland, had a mind to follow—a little roughly and crudely—the lines of the Ancient Mysteries concerning figurative death and resurrection. A signal confusion followed, for they slew the prototypical Master, whereas they raised the Candidate, creating a complete fissure in the logic of symbolism. So it has remained among us, but something like sixty years after the approximate date of construction, the *Loge de la Bienfaisance* at Lyons, which transmuted the RITE OF THE STRICT OBSERVANCE, intervened to save the situation, so far as French Masonry was concerned, and in the Grade of PERFECT MASTER of St Andrew they raised Hiram as Christ. If we pursue the subject of confusion from another point of departure, we know that—by the hypothesis of the Third Degree—the Temple of Solomon was left unfinished, like the legend itself, from which consideration of simple fact it follows that any completion of the Third Degree should take up the Hiramic myth at the point where its story broke off, and lead it to an end in symbolism.

Now we are familiar, and more familiar, with the affirmation concerning the ROYAL ARCH, which is (1) that it is not to be regarded as in any sense a further Degree superposed upon the Craft, but (2) rather as a completion of the whole. So far, however, from concluding the Hiramic myth it leaves unbridged in Ritual a gap of several centuries, understood as historical time, and jumps to an examination of certain legendary events connected with preliminaries to the building of the Second Temple in the days of Zerubbabel. It follows that the Third Degree—historically speaking—is a story without an end, like Carové's German romance, while the ROYAL ARCH is a prolegomenon to another story, which story is not to be found in Masonry.

The sense in which the one is supplementary to the other is a matter of the Secret Tradition, a formula of loss and recovery, according to which the Holy Order seeks to elevate the Craft out of a region of untinctured symbolism to the threshold of Divine Science. It could have been done in a logical manner, preserving all the unities, and it so happens that the necessary elements were ready to the hands of the symbolists, if we can suppose—as, I think, is possible—that certain so-called side-grades, or steps, were already existing in some primitive form. In this case, the ROYAL ARCH has been lifted out of a sequence to which it belongs essentially, and apart from which its real message is divided and confused, if it must not be called lost. My purpose is to collect the links of the broken chain and then join them up.

If the question be why does the Craft Candidate pass through a figurative experience which connotes the idea of death and then through a shadow of resurrection, the answer is that the god died and rose in the Ancient Mysteries, as in the great prototypical example which is that of Osiris. He was of the Divine Pantheon, and he returned thereto, as to former companions at once of toil and attainment. So also Iacchos was torn to pieces, but again he was restored to life; Tammuz died and rose; the dead Adonis was given back to the arms of Venus, even as Persephone to Demeter. If it be asked, on the other hand, why in the ROYAL ARCH there is a quest followed *ad interiora terræ* and a discovery consequent thereon, the answer is that this is precisely the thesis concerning the preservation of a Secret Tradition, which descended from Adam, of which Enoch was a notable custodian, which came down to the time of Solomon and is carried thereafter through several eloquent memorials of Masonic Rite. It was not invented by Masonry, and if I speak here only of the mythos in Israel it is not peculiar thereto, though it appears under other aspects in other regions of traditional lore. Before linking up briefly the chain of Ritual, it is necessary to make a proviso with respect to the sources.

They are texts of what I am accustomed to call the Greater Exile of Israel, being that of the Christian centuries, and they are three in number: (1) the TALMUD BABLI; (2) The TALMUD HIEROSOLYMÆ, and (3) The SEPHER HA ZOHAR. The last is the latest of all in respect of time, its final redaction being referred by scholarship to the 13th Century, though it contains old elements. It is the great text of the Secret Tradition in Israel, and this—according to the ZOHAR—began with Adam, for Latin theology and that which is termed Kabalism meet unawares, and seem to clasp hands over things appertaining to the hypothetical state of unfallen man in Paradise. It was a state of supernal knowledge, of the science which—by the theosophical hypothesis—has its root in the Tree of Life, in the unity of Divine things, not in the duality and sophistication which is referable to the Tree of Knowledge. It is said that when the Holy One, blessed be He, created Adam, He exhorted him to advance in the path of goodness and revealed to him the Mystery of Wisdom. Adam contemplated, indeed, all wisdom and all highest mysteries. He was 'encompassed by the glory from on high,' and was intended in the scheme of divine things to be united for ever with God in Whose Image he had been made. But from the path of the Good and the One—all this notwithstanding—Adam fell into ways of separation and abandoned the Tree of Life, meaning the supreme theosophy of the inward Secret Doctrine. The penalty of this separation is described under the term death in the text of Genesis.

By the hypothesis of the ZOHAR, the Secret Doctrine, the Supreme Wisdom, in a word, that Hidden Treasure which was transmitted in perpetuity thereafter as a tradition through the ages, was communicated to the First Man by means of a book, which came down from heaven in the hands of the angel Raziel, and was delivered to Adam, the messenger in question being denominated Chief of Supreme Mysteries. It remained in the possession of Adam till he was driven out of the Garden, when it was ravished out of his hands. But as it is obvious that there could have been no Secret Tradition—such as was conceived by the mind of Israel—unless its depository were restored, so we hear in due course that in answer to his tears and entreaties it was given back in the end to our progenitor by the angel Raphael. Adam transmitted it to Seth, from whom it passed to Enoch, who, after he was taken by God became the great angel Metatron, the Angel of the Presence and Chief of the Celestial School. It is said that the School of Metatron is the School of the Holy One, and that in his hands are the Keys of Heaven. It came about for these reasons that the Secret Book is called the BOOK OF ENOCH, though it passed down ultimately to Abraham. Thereafter the ZOHAR is silent regarding its travels and whereabouts, but the Secret Tradition of which it is the source was communicated to the elders by Moses and thence, in the myth concerning it, through succeeding generations to the doctors of the Zoharic school, the chief repository at the time of the fall of Jerusalem being Rabbi Simeon ben Yochai.

From Zoharic Kabalism the tradition descended to the follies and iniquities of Jewish Ceremonial Magic, and so it comes about that in these dregs and lees there is a BOOK OF RAZIEL, which is a book of Divine Names and Conjurations based thereon. It is a favourable specimen of its class, in comparison with Keys of Solomon, texts of Goëtia, Sworn Books of Honorius and things under the generic title of *Grimoires*; but it presents a corrupted form of the tradition concerning Enoch. Antecedent to the ZOHAR, as I have intimated, are certain Talmudic fables, which exceed the scope of this notice. Antecedent to both are Josephus and a comparatively ancient apocrypha of the apocalyptic class under the name of the BOOK OF ENOCH. To Josephus we owe the well-known myth concerning the Pillars of Stone and Brick, on which Enoch inscribed the Mysteries of Knowledge belonging to the age before the Flood: there are many variations of the legend, which concerns broadly the perpetuation of the Secret Tradition. It is not otherwise to our purpose. But the BOOK OF ENOCH, which is a series of visions beheld by the prophet when he was in the spirit, like the seer of Patmos, is a prototype of Masonic tradition and that especially which is reflected into the ROYAL ARCH. It is said that God shewed Enoch nine vaults in a vision, and that with the assistance of Methuselah his son, he proceeded to erect in the bosom of the mountain of Canaan a secret sanctuary, on the plan of what he had beheld, being vaults beneath one another.

In the ninth, or undermost, vault Enoch placed a triangle of purest gold, on which he had inscribed that which was presumably the heart, essence and centre of the Secret Tradition, the True Name of God, comprehending all grace, all power and the providence of Divine Mercy. It is the development of this legend which can be followed through several Grades and various Rites of Masonry, the root of all therein being referable to the Traditional History in the Third Craft Degree. We know that which it was attempted to wrest by violence from the keeping of the Master Builder: we know what he died to preserve inviolable, and though in reality it did not perish with him—because there were other Keepers—we know that Masonry suffered a loss through the centuries, and is represented as in the quest of its discovery in the Opening and Closing of the Lodge in the Master Grade. We know in fine what substitutes were accepted as distinctive tests, to prevail everywhere until in some manner as yet unknown the term of quest should be reached and the pearl of great price restored. When Moses, Aholiab and Bezaleel sat in the Holy Lodge, at the foot of Mount Horeb, during the long wanderings of Israel in the desert of Sinai, by the great hypothesis of the tradition, they were in plenary possession of all the Masonic treasure. When Solomon and others of the triad, who ruled the Sacred Lodge, sat on Mount Moriah, it was still as if the sun were at its meridian, a noon-tide glory of Masonry. But a change came over, by which the triad was broken and the light of the Art was obscured. It seems to me that in the deeper understanding our Craft Lodges are a memorial of this original loss: it is a logical inference from all that we are told in the story and from that which we claim to seek; for it is with us as it was with those Brethren of old, who, after the passing of the Master-Builder, agreed—till they could do better—to be content with things casual, though they desired things essential, and with accidents in place of the noumenal. It is as if, having heard and followed a great call, and been long on the quest of God, it came about that—for want of a term—we had to rest satisfied with His image, or with unconsecrated Bread and Wine in place of the Higher Eucharist and the Holy Grail.

But after nearly five hundred years—I am speaking still within the hypothesis of the symbolism—there rose up the Grand or Royal Lodge, which was in the day of restoration and the day when things are reborn or made anew, when Zerubbabel, the prince of the people, with their prophet and priest, led back Israel out of exile. It came about that, having made a great discovery within the precincts of the First Temple, they held their Lodge at Jerusalem, and proclaimed the glad tidings, which are called the climax of Freemasonry—at least within the measures and under the obedience of the Old Law. And the original of that which we term the ROYAL ARCH is the Grand or Royal Lodge. In the sense of this symbolism, notwithstanding all disparities occasioned by things that are left at a loose end and all temporal *lacunae*, it may be said that the Holy Order does, within its own degree, complete the Masonic circle—though only within measures of the Craft—in virtue of that mystical recovery which made the glory of the Third Grand Lodge even as the glory of the first, and Jerusalem in the days of Zerubbabel-as Horeb in those of Moses, who first promulgated the beneficent Law of Masonry.

The ROYAL ARCH may be defined briefly as the Grade of the Word attained; but while a certain expectation is intimated on the part of those who ruled, there is nothing to shew that the Brethren who made the discovery were qualified by antecedent knowledge or were themselves dedicated to the work of quest. It was the providence of an accidental happening which brought about the event, and as such—on the surface—it does litle honour to the important subject in hand. The discovery itself is unintelligible, as the story stands, since there is nothing leading up thereto—either in the Craft or Arch. But in Masonic Grades external to both, the preliminary steps are found and the motive at work throughout. In view of this fact, as explained already, it would look as though the ROYAL ARCH had been lifted out of some Ritual series and utilized as an epilogue to the Craft, not a little to its own detriment, because it was never intended originally to stand alone. In Masonic history we hear of the bare title and of some undescribed symbol belonging thereto being carried in a Masonic procession, *tempus* 1743, while a year later there is an allusion to the Grade itself, but under circumstances which suggest that more than one version was about. The prelimary side-steps or intermediates to which I have alluded and which throw light on the subject are not in distinct evidence till a later period. If I may put forward a personal opinion, purely at its hypothetical value, it seems to me that as the ROYAL ARCH originated in these islands, certainly and beyond question, so also there were other Grades, side-steps or preliminaries connected therewith and essential thereunto. It is impossible to speculate about their original form, in the absence of all evidence, or on how far they have departed from it in the Degrees now extant: if we may judge by the vicious editing of the Arch Degree itself, they have suffered drastic change. The Grades in question are called respectively ROYAL and SELECT MASTER. But before offering a brief description of their scope and motive I must refer to the year 1754, when several important items were grouped together under the auspices of a French Rite, as if they had been manufactured suddenly or suddenly collected together. I refer to the COUNCIL OF EMPERORS OF THE EAST AND WEST, otherwise the RITE OF HEREDOM or RITE OF PERFECTION, working twenty-two Grades superposed on those of the Craft. In virtue of certain sub-titles attached to some of them, on the authority of rare MSS. now in my hands, it would appear that not all of them were of French origin, though it is impossible to have any assurance on such a debatable point. The examples include ENGLISH MASTER, as alternative to INTIMATE SECRETARY, and ILLUSTRIOUS IRISH MASTER, as substitute for PROVOST AND JUDGE. However this may be, we are concerned more especially with the thirteenth Grade of the Rite, called ROYAL ARCH OF ENOCH, or—in early examples—Knight of the ROYAL ARCH. As there are two titles, so also there are two forms and that which is the more important is, I think, perhaps the later: it is incorporated at the present day into the long series of the SCOTTISH RITE. It goes very near to the root-hypothesis of the Secret Tradition and delineates the circumstance under which the Sacred Word was placed in the hiddenness, long prior to the Three Prototypical Grand Lodges. In this form, I believe it to be of foreign invention as well as redaction: its importance for our purpose is that it places a Masonic complexion on an early epoch of the Tradition. In the alternative and possibly earlier form there is no question that it is of English origin as to its root-matter or that it derives from the ROYAL and SELECT MASTER GRADES, but from the former more especially, and at a time when both were in a state corresponding more nearly to the mode in which they were communicated, not so many years ago, under the auspices of the EARLY GRAND SCOTTISH RITE, rather than that of the CRYPTIC. The latter bears marks of editing by persons who had no acquaintance with the Secret Tradition. As regards all recensions, the time is that of Solomon, the Temple is still uncompleted, but the mythical history in each case is subsequent to the Hiramic myth, which is still left at its original loose end. The Grades in their several forms throw light on the central point of the Royal Arch, because they shew how a place of concealment was planned for the Secret Mysteries and how these were hidden therein until time or circumstances should render their restoration essential. The implicit throughout is that in such case the providence protecting what is understood as Masonry would intervene in favour of the Art, as it did *ex hypothesi* at the epoch of the Second Temple.

We may follow the Secret Tradition into strange places of Masonry, and if the intimations are often at variance they are in agreement on at least two points. The Tradition is always concerned with the power and grace of a Word, usually a Divine Name, and there is always an intention to shew that a hidden Knowledge concerning it goes on from age to age. There is the Grade of KNIGHT OF THE EAST, which in one of its versions belongs to the Maccabean period, and the Candidate is in search of the Sacred Treasure after the profanations of Antiochus Epiphanus. There is the Grade of TRUE SCOTTISH MASTER, which belongs to Adonhiramite Masonry. It affirms that the Word of God was never lost in reality, and that after the sacking of Herod's Temple at the destruction of Jerusalem by Titus, a mysterious inscribed plate was found beneath one of the Pillars. This fable is recited in a kind of historical discourse, and although on the surface we are still in the days of Solomon, we are already on the threshold of Christian Masonry, for the Lodge of the Grade is said to have been instituted by St John the Evangelist in succession to one which was held on the banks of the Jordan by St John the Baptist.

When we pass definitely into Christian Masonry the Tradition is still with us, although under several mutations. It owes something to Philostorgus and his ECCLESIASTICAL HISTORY, written at the beginning of the 5th Century. In connection with the baffled attempts to rebuild the Temple at Jerusalem he tells us of certain workmen let down by means of ropes into a deep well, at the bottom of which—emerging above the water—there was found a small column, and on the column a book wrapped in a linen cloth. When examined, it proved to be a copy of St

John's Gospel. For the rest, according to Christian Masonry, the Keepers of the Secret Tradition are represented as Knights of the Morning, Knights of Palestine, Sons of the Valley, Thebaid Brethren, a secret Brotherhood perpetuated from generation to generation in the heart of Jewry, but unknown to Jewry at large. They looked for a Master who was to come, the Deliverer and Messiah. In the fullness of time they found the Word in Christ, which is the message of the Christian Grades.

I have been dealing with questions of fact in Ritual and with the tradition out of which they arise. I do not intend on the present occasion to dwell on the inferences to be drawn, however legitimate. I have followed the Secret Tradition in its development through several paths, within and outside of Masonry. That there is a meaning behind the Tradition I am entirely certain, for it is of symbolism or allegory after its own manner and within its own measures, even as Masonry is. The great BOOK OF THE ZOHAR contains the whole doctrine of the Lost Word and of the circumstances under which it shall be restored on the coming of Israel out of exile, in the day of Messiah. But the ZOHAR is the book of the Secret Tradition in Jewry under the Christian ægis. As regards the Lost Word, it depends from a question of fact, which of itself is of minor consequence, being the loss of the mode in which the High Priest pronounced the Divine Name when he entered the Holy of Holies once a year to make atonement for the sins of the people. Over this the ZOHAR allegorizes and in their fervid hearts the doctors of the Greater Exile looked for *magnalia Dei* when it should be put again into their mouths. But that which it meant in their symbolism was the coming of the Kingdom of God on earth—to the chosen people above all, but apparently by derivation from these to all tongues and tribes and peoples and nations. The secret Tradition was taken over by zealous scholars of Christendom during the 16th and 17th Centuries, and they sought to convince Jewry that all which was expected had come in Christ, that it was possessed by the Gentiles and might be enjoyed by them if they would turn their hearts to Him. This is the philosophy of the Tradition in brief and crude summary. But in another form and aspect, it is the philosophy of the Tradition in Masonry, which is another story of a Word in loss or hiddenness, and this fact, which might be one of coincidence, is linked up with the Secret Tradition because it is represented—

invariably and only—by a Sacred Name, an omnific and ineffable message, and the plenary grace of a mystery abiding in a Name of God. Now the Tradition of the Name in Masonry was taken over by other *Zelatores*. who, after all intimations of the ROYAL ARCH OF ENOCH, Arch of Zerubbabel and Arch of Josiah the King, after all that was said to be inscribed on sacred plates of gold, came forward in their later day and founded the Christian Grades—the ORDER OF THE TEMPLE, the ROSE CROIX, the RED CROSS OF CONSTANTINE and KNIGHT OF THE HOLY SEPULCHRE. Like other makers of legend, they testified that the Word is Christ. It follows that those rumours of a Secret Tradition which are conveyed in the Royal Arch are not confined thereto. In one or other form, they are in the body-general of Masonry.

What does this fact signify, and where may it lead the Mason who is willing to dwell on such things and, perhaps, pursue them further? The answer to this question is my last word and a kind of *obiter dictum*. It signifies that the Secret of Masonry, that Word too often lost, is the Secret of Christ realized in the heart of the Mason, and that from beginning to end 'our peculiar system of morality, veiled in allegory and illustrated by symbols' has never had another object than to direct us with eyes uplifted to the bright Morning Star, whose rising brings peace and salvation to those who sit in tribulation and in the shadow of death.

# 3
# ROBERT FLUDD AND FREEMASONRY: A SPECULATIVE EXCURSION

In any consideration of the possible connection between Freemasonry and the Rosicrucian movement, the figure of Robert Fludd (1574–1637) looms large. Waite had written on Fludd as early as 1894, but his more considered views appeared in the lecture *Robert Fludd and Freemasonry* that he delivered to the Manchester Association for Masonic Research in September 1921 (printed in the *Transactions* of the Association in the following year). It was revised—principally by the addition of extended footnotes—for *Emblematic Freemasonry*, but I have chosen to include the original version instead, as it conveys more clearly than does the expanded text the style of Waite's lectures.

I OPEN the speculative consideration of this paper with a statement which may appear drastic, but it represents my conclusions at their value on the subject of Masonic Research. After more than one generation of earnest and highly qualified inquiry, introduced by a much longer period of reverie and invention, we are still in the dark upon those circumstances under which Speculative Masonry originated as a system of morality presented in the form of Ritual, protected by covenants of silence, making claims upon a remote past and veiling its instructions by recourse to allegory and symbolism. We know only too well about the old dreams which every man of sense, within and without the Order, has set aside long since, and the recitation of which at this day can only sound ridiculous. It seems almost incredible that people posing as serious should have ever affirmed, as they did, that Masonry was older than the world, because the Great Architect of the Universe, by virtue of His work in the cosmos, was assuredly the first Freemason; that alternatively it began with Adam in Paradise, though he does not seem to have made even his own coat of skin; and so forward through a heavy cloud of false and dull imaginings. These clouds have melted. We have emerged also more or less from those mists of invention, a typical example of which proposed that the Tower of Babel was the work of early speculative craftsmen, whose hands are to be traced also in the Pyramids of Egypt, in the Temples of Solomon and Zerubbabel, and—broadly speaking—in all ancient monuments of the Building Art. The hypothesis was that the old architects, stonemasons, wallers, paviours and plasterers were all in some mysterious manner not only material and operative artists, but moralists, ritualists and makers of mystery-symbolism. The *a priori* argument in support of this view is obviously that our Speculative Masonry is an art of building spiritualized, or more accurately is that art figuratively and morally transformed and applied—from which is might seem to follow that it arose among building craftsmen. The valid condemnation, however, arises from the fact that there is no particle of evidence anywhere in the world of the past to indicate that the old architects and builders had any notions of moralities veiled in allegory or illustrated by symbols. The records of this view are prolonged through several generations of Masonic *literati* and have come down to us and are with us implicitly in much of the qualified and admirable work of modern research. To throw new light on architecture, on building guilds, is still in some vague and undeclared manner expected to promote knowledge of our purely emblematic subject. The research has produced valuable results within its own measures, but nothing in respect of our concern. There are still studious and greatly serious people—among whom I must count that excellent Mason and my dear friend, Brother Joseph Fort Newton—who think that Leader Scott—otherwise, Mrs Baxter—made a substantial contribution to the antiquities of Speculative Masonry in her work on the Cathedral Builders.\* She made no contribution to anything except the history of architecture. There are others whose eyes have turned—as my own turned eagerly, and not so far in the past—towards Old Charges and Constitutions. But a century and more of these valuable documents have not given us one

---

\* See *The Builders: A Story and Study of Masonry*, 1915, pp. 87 et seq.

line of help, from the Regius MS onward to the first years of the eighteenth century.

This is how the case stands in respect of what I must call legitimate or authorized research. The fantasiasts are still among us, making great claims and clothed in all the vestures of dogmatic certitude. Their appeal is to Egypt, Babylon, India, Mexico, Peru, Yucatan, wheresoever the building monuments of ancient civilization remain to testify, wheresoever there are figured moments and records of primeval inscription. The recurrence of certain simple signs and symbols, recalling those of Masonry or identical therewith, are no evidence of our moral and spiritual art of building in those ages and places. If it could be shewn conclusively that a secret society flourishing 5,000 BC communicated between its members by means of our Craft signs it would be a point of curious interest, but it would prove nothing. To affirm Speculative Masonry, *e.g.*, in Egypt, is to affirm our highly conventional system of morality, illustrated by building symbols and a building myth. Still less does it help any thesis of antiquity to cite the existence from time immemorial and the almost universal prevalence of the triangle, square, pentagram, hexagram and other geometrical symbols. The antecedent fact of these figures can prove nothing to us as Masons, apart from their particular application, as this prevails among us. Assuredly these points of simple and obvious criticism must have been advanced by others before me: they may be commonplaces of our curious research, yet their repetition is imposed because we have by no means emerged from the extravagance of Masonic assumption.

It follows that there is still no answer to the recurring question: When, where and how did Symbolical Masonry arise? A hundred voices have answered in at least as many ways, but not one of them has had any cards of evidence to lay upon the table in support of any thesis. In such cases it means usually that a given subject has been begotten ready made and armed, like Minerva out of the brain of some creative Jupiter, whether an individual or a company. If this is the solution of our problem, most of us know where to look on the hither side of the year 1717. It is in the direction of Desaguliers, as a possible shaper of the Craft Degrees into something approaching broadly the form in which we have them now. But in this case it does not follow that he made up out of his own head the entire emblematic aspects of Masonry, as well as the ritual aspects. The question in my mind is whether something of this kind may have come into his hands and whether we can indicate, however tentatively, a possible source in the past, seeing that all the known avenues have failed us in the course of our research.

There is one which I have not mentioned and which has stood so far in no better position than the rest. When the German Rosicrucians of the late eighteenth century adopted a Masonic aspect by communicating their Mysteries to applicants in the guise of a formal Rite, they defined their Masonic position by affirming that our Speculative Brotherhood owed its existence to themselves.* It was a dogmatic claim, to be taken or left as one chose, seeing that the problematical Order was not in the habit of producing evidence for its statements, at least on the historical side. I do not find that the affirmation had any effect on Freemasonry, which, so far as the Continent is concerned, was in the midst of many competitors pretending to the same position of fatherhood; but at the beginning of the nineteenth century, the Rosicrucian origin of the Craft, was advanced seriously by J. G. Buhle,† though he shewed no first-hand acquaintance with the Rite to which I have referred. The hypothesis passed over to France, where it found a champion in Reghellini,‡ speaking in terms of certitude, whereas Buhle argued a thesis and sought to produce his reasons. In 1853 Ragon§ went still further and presented the Craft grades as manufactured by a Rosicrucian in the middle of the seventeenth century, some seventy-five years before they came into being. It is also an old story in England, for Thomas de Quincey** dressed up Buhle's argument and presented it in a series of papers which

* The claim appears more especially in certain very rare and almost unique Rituals, the MSS of which are in my possession. They belong to the period circa 1777 and are of great importance in the later history of the Rosy Cross.

† *Ueber den Ursprung . . . der Rosenkreuzer und Freymaurer*, 1804.

‡ *La Maçonnerie, considérée comme la résultat des Religions Egyptienne, Juive et Chrétienne*, 1833.

§ *Orthodoxie Maçonnique*.

** His Essay was first published in *The London Magazine*, Vol. IX.

belong to literature. It became the fashion of a period with several later dreamers. There is no question also that it captivated the alert and careful mind of Robert Freke Gould, though he saw plainly enough that Buhle, Nicolai, Ragon and a dozen who followed their lead did not prove their case. Gould was tentative enough and far away from any belief on the subject, but he was manifestly drawn and impressed, while that which impressed and drew him was the primary fact that at Warrington in 1646 Elias Ashmole, supposed Rosicrucian and known alchemist and hermetist, was made a Mason and thought enough of the matter to attend a second meeting, but this time in London, some sixteen years subsequently. Nor this only for he had planned and collected certain materials towards a History of Masonry, by which, however, must be understood the building art and not a figurative mystery which teaches men to be good by means of symbols and an allegorical myth.

What kind of Lodge it was that met at Warrington we are never likely to know, except that it admitted to membership persons who were not Operative Masons and was ruled apparently by a Warden. It is moderately certain by the evidence of Ashmole's Diary that he never revisited the city and that he did not attend any other Lodge till the year 1682, when he was summoned to a meeting at Mason's Hall. He went there as a Fellow and, moreover, as the oldest present Brother of that rank. It seems to follow that if there were two Degrees in his day he received them on the same night, or alternatively—if there was only one—that he became a Fellow by the fact of his initiation. In this connection we may remember that the conventional title of Entered Apprentice seems to have been brought by Desaguliers from Scotland, though the Old English Charges recognize Apprentices and Fellows. There is another point of consequence which follows from the evidence of the Diary: the fact that he had been admitted at Warrington entitled Ashmole to attend a Lodge held in the Hall of the Masons' Company. Was it an ordinary Lodge, in which case the Company was practising the admission of non-operative members? Or was it that mysterious body, on which so much may hang, about which we know so little and are likely to learn no more—I mean, the Acception?* The Company has no records

---

\* See Conder's *Records of the Hole Craft and Fellowship of Masonry*, 1894.

prior to the fire of London—in which its archives were destroyed—except an Account Book, to which we owe our knowledge of the bare facts (1) that there was an Acception, (2) that it held Meetings distinct from those of the Company, and (3) that one might be a Master of the Masons' Company and would be yet ineligible as such to frequent Acceptance gatherings without passing through the Ceremony of Acception, whatever it was. On the one hand, it is possible hypothetically that Ashmole attended a meeting of this body because it appears to have been in existence at this date, in which case the Lodge at Warrington must have been a branch Lodge of the Acception, for the reason given—that the latter did not admit ordinary Masons, even if Masters of the Company. On the other hand, there is no evidence that the Lodge at Warrington was anything but an ordinary Lodge. We know, therefore, only that Ashmole was made a Mason, being a non-operative, and that long afterwards he was called to a Meeting at Masons' Hall, when he was in a position of seniority as regards the rest of the Fellows.

It follows that the case of Ashmole does not offer us any colourable ground for a Rosicrucian hypothesis in respect of Masonry, more especially as there is no shred of evidence that he ever belonged to any Rosicrucian School or Order. He had thought in alchemy till he spoke in its own tongue and it spoke like a language to him. But all Rosicrucians were not alchemists, while very few alchemists indeed were connected with the Rosy Cross. There is in fact only one great name, which is that of Michael Maier, and he belonged to the literature of the subject, rather than to its art or science.* To this extent the Ashmole case must be called a manifest delusion, and it is difficult to understand how it captivated anyone; but for people like Gould it connoted the school of Hermetic thought in England and dreams about Francis Bacon, the Pillars of Hermes, the New Atlantis, and the beginnings of the Royal Society, in which the Hermetic School had a part of membership.

It happens, however, that the case of possible hermetic and even Rosicrucian influence on the rise of Emblematic Freema-

---

\* In addition to his purely alchemical works, such as *Atalanta Fugiens*, he wrote *Silentium post Clamores* in defence of the Rosicrucian Order, and a Commentary on the Laws of the Brotherhood, being those published in *Fama Fraternitatis* R ∴ C ∴

sonry does not stand or fall with Ashmole. Let us take the fact of the Acception—more mysterious, if possible, than the Rosy Cross—some twenty-six years behind the Warrington episode, or to the date under which it is mentioned first in the Account Book of the Mason's Company, namely, 1620. The Manifestoes of the Rosy Cross appeared in Germany onward from the year 1614. In 1616 and 1617, when a great debate on the subject was proceeding at full course in that country, there had appeared at Leyden a Latin defence of the Order under the name of Robertus de Fluctibus. It came out in two divisions, the preface to the text as *Apologia Compendiaria*, a minute independent pamphlet, and then the work itself, or *Tractatus Apologeticus*, with the preface thereto reprinted. The author was Robert Fludd, whose ancestral home was a beautiful manorial house at Bearstead, Kent, a few miles from Maidstone. He had also a residence in London, close by the headquarters of the Masons' Company, otherwise in Coleman Street. Fludd was born in 1576 and died on September 8th, 1637. I do not propose to speak of his external life, which is well known, but it may be noted that he was in Germany and elsewhere on the Continent for several years prior to 1605, when he graduated in medicine at Oxford. It is reasonable to suppose that much of his profound theosophical, metaphysical and occult knowledge was acquired abroad.

Let me assure you at this point that I am not proposing to contribute a further *dossier* to the archives of mendacity concerning the Rosy Cross. It must be understood, as my sub-title states, that this is only a speculative excursion, the consideration of a purely possible case which is not, I fear, likely to emerge in the realm of certitude. It is an interesting fact that Fludd was on his travels during what may be called the Rosicrucian formative period, or from 1598, when the *Militia Crucifera Evangelica* held their Congress at Luneburg, to 1604, when Simon Studion completed his *avant courier* of all the symbolism in his vast unprinted treatise, *Naometria*.\* Were I the spokesman of occult societies, formulating matters of reverie in terms of alleged fact, I should proclaim in all their colleges that Fludd attended this memorable if obscure meeting; that he was acquainted with Studion and was by him brought within the

---

\* See *Wirtgembergisches Repertorium du Litteratur*, 3 vols, 1782–3.

ranks of the *Militia*, that he saw and talked with the famous Johannes Valentinus Andrea—alleged Founder of the Rosy Cross—then a precocious boy in his teens. As it is, I remember only that Fludd's acquired and natural dedications were after the manner born of those to which the Order itself confessed. Whatever he acquired in Germany or elsewhere on the Continent, was supplemented by further study in the pleasant solitude of Bearstead and amidst his medical practice in London. He was forty years old in 1616 and had matured his views. His apology for the Rosy Cross, being his first appearance in print, is typical in every way of his mental outlook, his curious occult learning and the extravagance by which he was characterized. It may have brought him to the notice of like-minded people abroad and possibly to a few at home. It was the beginning of a literary life which was devoted throughout to the development of what may be called, in a broad sense, the principles and philosophy connoted by the word Rosicrucian. The cosmos and microcosmos were treated in his folios from the standpoint of Kabalism, the Higher Magia, Alchemy and Hermetic Medicine. There is no opportunity to speak of them here, and no need arises. He is ridiculous enough in his reveries and his credulity knew no bounds, but he had read widely within the limits of his concerns and he had thought at first hand upon them, so that he is in no sense a man who merely reflected others or who produced works of compilation. His books were published abroad; there is no question that they were known and read: indeed the best evidence that they were things that mattered at their period, in the opinion of their period, is that men like Mersennus and Gassendus wrote volumes in reply to his own. For the rest, his writings exhibit him as a man of intellectual tenacity and personal force who would count among those about him, and would have to be reckoned with at need. He seems to me likely to have drawn round him a certain circle at a period such as that of King James I, more especially as he was known at court, was one of the court physicians and—as he testifies on his own part—was favoured by that Monarch.

Such being the case as regard Robert Fludd, let us now recur to the Acception. My hypothesis concerning it is (1) that this Association or Lodge differed *in toto* from any Lodge of Operative Masonry, and this is certain, because the highest attainable position in the Masons' Company, being that of

Master, did not carry—as we have seen—any right to attend its meetings, without being joined on formally, or in other words 'accepted'; (2) that the kind of difference did not correspond to that of an Operative Lodge which received members outside the operative trades, as, *e.g.*, the Lodge at Warrington in 1646, which according to Ashmole's Diary may have included both classes; (3) that at the same time it connected sufficiently with or so far favoured Masons that it made them eligible and received them on a smaller scale of fees, as shewn in the Account Book of the Masons' Company; (4) that it was about some other business and that a key to its nature may be indicated by Robert Fludd, when in a manifest Rosicrucian connection he speaks of a House Mystic built up of living stones, of ascending a *Mons Rationabilis*, which Mountain was a Way to Christ, while Christ was the corner-stone of the spiritual building represented by the other symbolism. The Acception, in a word, was—I think—precisely like a certain Secret Order which met continuously at Mark Masons' Hall for a period of about twenty years, or up to the year 1914, and accepted Masons, among many others, as members, which worked in Ritual, and was to this extent under the Masonic ægis, but had otherwise no connection therewith. There is very full material at need for the history of this Association, should a necessity arise: were it otherwise, in a century to come, so far as Mark Masonry is concerned, it might be known only by an Account Book, a bare record in ledgers concerning fees paid, under a certain heading, for a considerable period. It happens, to complete my case, if not to institute a strict fine parallel, that the body in question was Hermetic and perhaps Rosicrucian in character.

Now, knowing as I do in a reasonably intimate manner the records of Robert Fludd, my suggestion is that in the year 1620 we may not have to look much further than the Kentish theosophist to explain how the Acception came into being and that for which it stood. I have intimated that Fludd was not the kind of man who was likely to store his light under figurative bushels, and through all his life he was about the business of his particular dedications and interests. There are two points of view possible as regards his connection with the Brotherhood of the Rosy Cross, being (1) that at some unassignable date after the publication of his *Apologia* he was made a member, which would, as it seems to me, have come about only by emissaries of the Order visiting England for the purpose of his reception, or (2) that he constituted himself its dogmatic interpreter on the faith of its published documents. In the first case, his initiation would not be referable to Michael Maier, about whose connection with Fludd several scandalous mendacities have been put forward in recent years, though it could serve little purpose to expose them in this place. Maier was a great German alchemist of the early seventeenth century, but apparently—as I have said—of the literary rather than of the practical kind. It seems to me, I mean, that he produced his theories of the work in obscure parables and allegories, but they belong to the study rather than to the laboratory. It is certain in any case that he was over in England antecedently to the year 1616-17, and it is quite possible that he met Fludd, but it would be prior to the *Apologia*, when Fludd was utterly unknown, while Maier himself was no great name in the world, for he was at the beginning only of his brief but exceedingly productive career in Hermetic literature. We do not know, but there is little reason to assume that he was then a member of the Rosy Cross, supposing that it was a corporate foundation in any institutional sense. Fludd, on the other hand, had little outside the learning which he was still in the course of acquiring, and there is no real evidence that he ever saw Maier. Supposing at some later date, and under circumstances about which we must be content to speculate in the dark, that he was integrated in the Rosy Cross, I register my conviction on the basis of his record at large that he would have been no inactive member. He was ever in the arena of book-production, armed at all points to uphold and defend the Order, and that which he did with the pen he is certain to have done also by word of mouth and by his personal influence among those about him. He would have had therefore his circle. There came a time in his writings when he, who in the valediction attached to his *Apologia* had pleaded for consideration and favour on the part of those whose cause he had espoused, began to speak with a certain authority concerning the Order, and even intimated changes that had taken place within it. There came a time when its purpose, dedication and concern were raised in his expositions into a purely spiritual sphere, so that it passed from the occult order of things, their monstrosities and crudities, in the direction of mystical doctrine. The fact of his initiation is not an arbitrary inference from his later

memorials, more especially as his personal good faith cannot be
called in question by those who know him at first hand. He was a
Christian theosophist, dedicated in heart and mind to Divine
things, as he was given to understand them. I speak of course on
the hypothesis that there was something corporate into which he
could be admitted, however informally such reception might
require to be understood at the period. In this connection the
counsel is one of caution. We are apt to judge every Secret
Order of the past according to the formal standards of Masonic
procedure. We picture immediately a Lodge, Chapter or
Temple which was opened and closed in a manner corresponding to that which prevails among us, which had a more or less
elaborate ceremonial for the initiation and advancement of
candidates, and a binding pledge with heavy penal clauses.
There is no trace of Ritual procedure in the Rosicrucian Order
prior to the year 1710, and then it is a mere vestige. The first
manifesto, called *Fama Fraternitatis*,\* indicates, almost unawares
and casually, that postulants promised to be secret and that
when they were passing through a period which corresponds to
the notion of a novitiate they 'performed their school,' or in
other words, went through a course of training. But Fludd was
trained already and had performed school enough in long years
of research which led up to his memorable folios, full of occult
learning if not of occult knowledge, and in the course of which
he spiritualized most things that pass under the dubious and
disdainful name of occult science. Given the hypothesis that he
was joined on to the Order, it would have been with little or next
to nothing of a defined, conventional kind. He would have been
received much as the Protestant persuasions represented by the
Confession of Augsburg would have recognized those who
subscribed to it intellectually and polemically as members of
their particular body. We cannot carry back the Order under any
circumstances further than the year 1604, which is the date of
the unprinted *Naometria*, under the name of Simon Studion,
but the earlier we can place it the less will it belong to ritual. It is
quite certain that whatever group of *literati* put forward the *Fama*

---

\* *Fama Fraternitatis des Loblichen Ordens des Rosenkreuzes an alle Gelehrte
und Häupter Europa geschrieben*, etc. Cassel, 1614. There were several
editions.

and *Confessio*\* were under nothing other than the rule of a common understanding and that they devised their traditional history concerning Christian Rosy Cross as an illustration of their claim in outline. By the hypothesis, they had something to impart under the veil of this pretence, and in proportion as their sincerity was greater, it is the more likely that it was or became an understanding and exposition of things occult in the sense of things spiritual, for the liberation and rescue of those who had been misdirected by the 'rogues and runagates' of common commercial Alchemy and Magia. From this point of view there is no question that Robert Fludd was of and belonged to the Order long years before it is antecedently likely that he entered one of its groups.

So far as regards the first case that I have cited, and in respect of the second I have only to say that he had dwelt so long upon the subject with perfervid zeal that as a man of position and influence, as well as a King's physician, he is peculiarly likely to have drawn others about him. There may have arisen in this manner an informal association of a Hermetic and Rosicrucian kind, just as in the days of Ashmole there was an informal grouping of astrologers, who had an annual feast together. It would have been tinctured deeply by the personal views and influence of him who led it and would have been a Rose-Cross circle with the ostensible German claims changed over in the light of his Christian spirit. It may not have affirmed a formal connection with any Brotherhood abroad, for it is unlikely that a relation of this kind would have carried the notion of importance which might attach to it for us at this day. It would have taken the traditional history of the *Fama* in some kind of literal sense, much as the Hiramic myth, though an evident allegory in which a morality was taught, came to be regarded from an historical standpoint in the quixotic quests of early Masonic explorers. It would have pondered over Rosicrucian parables concerning *Mons Magorum Invisibilis*, with a hidden Temple on its summit which could be entered only by those who were called and chosen. It would have discussed Alchemy in the spirit of *Summum Bonum* and *Clavis Philosophiæ Fluddanæ*, which had left any physical work altogether behind, had broken the alembics and shut the laboratories up, and was concerned with the corner-

---

\* The *Confessio Fraternitatis* R∴C∴ appeared in 1615.

stone and the *latens Deitas* of Christ Mystical; or—as Fludd terms it—with a 'Spiritual Chemistry' and 'gold of God'. In a word, it would have been a little group of 'philosophers by fire', such as Anthony à Wood might have loved to discourse about, with the characteristic ineptitudes of *Athenæ Oxonienses*. The minutes of their proceedings would be pearls of great price for our keeping, though I do not intend to suggest that as regards the real subject their debates would have been other than 'about it and about', for after all the ages the essence and the heart of this have still escaped expression. It would have been the same precisely had the head of the Hermetic House been initiated by Maier or another according to the manner born of *Leges Fraternitatis* R∴C∴.. I am quite certain that, however they dealt in mystery, dark as Trithemius or 'the more dark Libanius Gallus', the early Rosicrucians had nothing to tell their novices or adepts on 'the subject of the Art' which was of better worth or could profit them more than could Robert Fludd at his best. Moreover, and it is not without importance, unlike the Rosicrucian co-heirs in Germany, there would have been no anti-papal ranters among them and no hot gospels baked in post-Lutheran ovens. Fludd was an English gentleman with a catholic heart in a coat of the liberal Anglican fashion.

This is the kind of association which may have met under the name of Acception at the Hall of the Masons' Company from 1620 onward, a few metaphorical yards from the house of Robert Fludd, and this is how it may have arisen. Its foundation does not of necessity belong, however, to the year mentioned, which is that of its first appearance in the book of records. It was not of necessity started by Robert Fludd, but if anything brought him within it, he would have changed it. However it arose, my thesis is that the Acception was not impossibly a group of Hermetic students, of which there were many at the period, that Fludd drew them together or took his place among them, and that after this manner, and the manner of the Rosy Cross, they began to speak of spiritual building in a Hall of Masons, of a Hermetic Art in stone, and that in this way they contributed something to a figurative art of building. It came about that Fludd died in his day, and —if my dream is true—the Acception lost its master. It continued, however, and began to draw Masons within it: they may have been in it in his own day. There came a time when a Master of the Company did actually join them, paid his fees and probably ate his dinners. The days went on, and it may be that the Hermetic element faded, as the Operative element dissolved in the Company itself. It is not heard of after 1680, but owing to its admixture of Masons, operative and non-operative, with men of its own concern, any speculative elements within it would have done their work. The Rosicrucian counsel: *Transmutemini, transmutemini de lapidibus mortuis in lapides vivos philosophicos*, would have been familiar among them in another manner of language, and in the likeness of the 'house not made with hands, eternal in the heavens' they may have laid certain foundations of the emblematic house of Masonry. The prototypical symbolism would be that of Robert Fludd on the building of a House of Wisdom, an emblematical temple of man, a spiritual palace on the mountain and a House of the Rosy Cross.

This is my thesis, Brethren, to be taken or left at will. It is, if you like, the shewing of a vision, a speculative excursion in an open field. As it seems to me, I have indicated that there is a possible source at least from which a Masonic typology may have been derived as to its roots by him or them who constructed the Craft Degrees, *post* 1717. I have offered also a new and reasonable manner of regarding the once alleged influence of the Rosy Cross on the development of Freemasonry, as known and practised among us.

# 4
# HERMETIC SCHOOLS AND MASONRY

Waite's attitude to the relationship between Freemasonry and Hermeticism is well illustrated by two of the entries in his *New Encyclopaedia of Freemasonry* (1921) which are here combined under the title he gave to the first of them. The second entry, *Kabalistic Tradition and Masonry*, follows naturally from the first as the Kabalah is the final Hermetic School of the three which Waite considers. The original versions of the two essays were revised for the projected second edition of the *Encylopaedia* which was never published (the so-called 'New and revised edition' is, in fact, simply a reprint of the first edition), and it is Waite's revised texts that are now printed for the first time.

IF WE isolate the Building Guilds of the Middle Ages and later from all imputed correspondence—by way of descent—with the Ancient Mysteries, with Dionysians and Essenes, Roman Collegia and Crusading Knights, or Solomon and his Temple; if we take them just as they are, acknowledging that their history is still in cloud and darkness for want of sufficient materials to elucidate it, but supposing that they originated—like other trade unions—as a matter of trade convenience or trade necessity; if we picture them as craftsmen in stone and clay, somewhat roughly banded together; it is still indubitable that out of these Guilds a Speculative Fraternity was either evolved in modern days or another and emblematical concern was superposed thereon. At a given period and in an undetermined place something occurred so to transfigure these artificers that they ceased gradually to hew stones, to make bricks, to plan and to build edifices; that they laid down chisel and hammer, assumed the mantle of philosophers and began to concern themselves—theoretically at least—in the progress of humanity, the improvement of its moral nature, and in that which is termed loosely a spiritual experiment. How this came about is the problem which remains for our consideration and for solution, if that be possible.

**Three Hermetic Schools.** In earlier days of research—the eighteenth century and onward—Emblematic Freemasonry was taken on its own terms. The makers of all the spurious histories, the dreamers of all the fond, romantic dreams—both here and on the Continent—ignored to all intents and purposes the historical distinction between an Operative and a Speculative mode. Was Masonry before the world in God? Did it date from Adam in Paradise? Was the first Lodge opened in Egypt? However the thesis shaped it was Speculative Masonry worked in Three Degrees, having no essential distinction from those which obtain among us; and it was as much in vogue among artists who built the Pyramids, Babel or Solomon's Temple as it was among Essenes and Thebaid hermits, who built only in the heart. When other counsels of research obtained in England and abroad it became, as we have seen, a custom to explore the records of the Building Guilds. I do not know whether I am the first to say that this quest has failed, but I have not come across my precursor. The multiplication of old Charges and analogous documents, the tabulation of their variants, the criticism of spurious codices have exercised great skill and deserve all praise, being invaluable for the history of architecture; but as to origin or development, Emblematic Freemasonry remains substantially where it was—a considerable Dramatic Mystery with its origin in the clouds. In respect of documentary evidence, we know as little whence it came as those who profess it among us know whither it is going. Under these circumstances we seem led irresistibly to infer that it originated where and when it was first manifested, being the City of London in the early eighteenth century. But it happens that there is one direction which has been regarded not unfavourably as a possible source of light. It is that of the Hermetic Schools in England, and these—speaking broadly—may be classified as three—Alchemical, Rosicrucian and Kabalistic. They had a common bond of interest and tended, here as elsewhere, to merge into a single school.

**Symbolic Groups.** The presence of a non-operative element among Masons at an early period has been suggested by several writers. Mr R. F. Gould considers that we are justified in inferring that from the fourteenth century, or even earlier, there were associations of a speculative or symbolic character, as apart from practical Masonry, though—with the sincerity by which he was characterized—he adds that on this point the judgment of certain students was opposed to his own. We have seen on our own part that the view is unsupported by evidence. On the other hand, the practice of receiving within the ranks of the Fraternity men who were neither architects nor builders, and that not merely as patrons, is beyond challenge. This practice was characteristic, however, of most Trade Guilds in England. Now, the hypothesis with which I am concerned suggests that the Hermetic Schools intervened for the transfiguration of English Operative Masonry about the middle of the seventeenth century. The Reformation had succeeded the Renaissance, and with all the disabilities attaching to both movements there can be no doubt that there was a great extension of the intellectual horizon. Many new avenues of thought had been thrown open, and men, being comparatively free to speak and act, acted and spoke freely, within the limits of their opportunities, while among other things there was a new impulse in Germany and England given to the prosecution of several branches of inquiry which antecedently could have been and were pursued only at the personal peril of the student. In England the practical experiment of Alchemy was undertaken by numerous persons, and it is just prior to the date which I have mentioned that the rumour of the ROSICRUCIAN FRATERNITY raised curiosity in Europe. Hermetic literature—not only with a modern accent but almost for the first time in vernacular languages—extended greatly, and schools of Theosophy sprang up in several countries. The root of the Rosicrucian movement was in Germany, but the impulse reached England, and some of the most famous names connected with the subject are identified with this country. Hence came Alexander Seton and hence Eirenæus Philalethes, who has been regarded as one of the great masters of Hermetic Art. Here also was Robert Fludd, who must—I think—be regarded as not only advocate and apologist in chief of the Rosicrucian Art and Philosophy but as a fountain-head. Here too was Thomas Vaughan—mystic as well as alchemist. And here in 1640 lived Elias Ashmole, alchemist and antiquary—founder also of the Ashmolean Museum at Oxford.

**English Alchemists.** There are evidences to shew that the experiment of Alchemy in England was at the period of Ashmole an exceedingly old pursuit. It was practised certainly in the time of Chaucer, but the literary remains of the early period are non-existent rather than scanty. Vernacular manuscripts date, broadly speaking, from about the fifteenth century, and Roger Bacon is perhaps the first name which can be cited in connection with the subject. As regards printed books prior to the seventeenth century, these also are few and far between, but no doubt there were many practical processes derived from Latin treatises, and they would have come over chiefly from Germany. At the beginning of the seventeenth century there must have been a great awakening of interest, though it is clear from evidence furnished personally by Robert Fludd that his own voluminous writings—several of which bear indirectly on this subject—found a considerable public abroad, and next to none at home. The interest grew, however, and must have been diffused rather widely before the middle of the seventeenth century. It was maintained and stimulated by visitors from abroad, some of whom claimed to possess important secrets of Rosicrucian and Hermetic Art. In the face of possibilities opened by such pretensions, but following also the general tradition of the literature—and taught, moreover, like others, by the experience of their own failures—English students came to regard this Art as a Secret transmitted rather than as a Mystery that could be acquired by the pains of untutored research; and one result of this feeling would be the association of pupils under the guidance of an adept or master—real or supposed.

**Alchemical Groups.** In this way also informal alchemical associations may have come into being, but they have left no trace behind them. It should be added that the horizon of Alchemy in England was more limited than in some of its developments abroad, where its traditions came almost to rival the so-called universal science of Raymond Lully. By means of Hermetic Art men hoped in England to transmute metals and to produce an elixir which would heal diseases and prolong life. When they sought after these secrets, and when they wrote concerning them, there is little evidence of any ulterior object in view, of Spiritual Alchemy as it was understood by Heinrich Khunrath and Jacob Böhme, or of the catholic concern of Paracelsus at an earlier date. Now, it is precisely in the seventeenth century that we meet with traces of a change in this respect, beginning with Robert Fludd, and when Thomas Vaughan wrote his strange little books on the subject Alchemy in England was coming slowly into touch with a wider spirit of research—as it was pursued, for example, in Germany—and was assuming something of that accent and intention which help to connect it—as it does connect undoubtedly—with certain broad aspects of the initiatory process.

**Operative and Speculative Masonry**. A section of Masonic opinion has looked in the past and a section looks still towards Elias Ashmole and his connections as in some way—yet undetermined—the representatives of the transition from Operative to Speculative Masonry. In France there has been practically no doubt on the subject from the days of Ragon, though concerning the value of his personal view I have spoken with desirable plainness elsewhere in this section. In America the distinguished name of Albert Pike can be cited in support of the thesis. After every allowance has been made for the position of such a speculation, still almost inextricable, it can be affirmed at least that it might offer a place of repose for all the tolerable views, because it harmonizes all—on the understanding that Ashmole and his consociates are not regarded personally but as typifying a leavening spirit introduced there and here, and at work during the period intervening between 1640 and the foundation of the first Grand Lodge in 1717. It would account at once not alone for Hermeticism itself but for alleged Rosicrucian influence as a part thereof, for the obvious presence of Kabalistic elements in Speculative Masonry, and for all other contributories of an esoteric character in the symbols and legends of the Fraternity, as well as for that otherwise incomprehensible bond of sympathy which—in the eighteenth century and onward for one hundred and more years—subsisted between Masonry and the purely occult societies, and which developed at one period a most striking sequence of results, as we shall see in its place later on. Pike was like Ragon unfortunately, a man of uncritical mind, and I summarize his findings under all needful reserves.

**Hermetic and Masonic Symbols**. Among Masonic symbols which he identifies as used in common by Freemasons and Hermetic and Alchemical literature are the Square and Compasses, the Triangle, the Oblong Square, the Legend of the Three Grand Masters, the idea embodied in a substituted Word—which may well be the most important of all—together with the Sun, the Moon and Master of the Lodge. It was, moreover, his opinion, based on this and other considerations, that the Philosophers—meaning in his case the members of Hermetic Confraternities—became Freemasons and introduced into Masonry their own symbolism. He thinks finally that Ashmole was led to be made a Mason because others who were followers of Hermes had taken the step before him.

**Hermetic Literature**. Unfortunately it is very nearly impossible in the existing state of our knowledge to set forth even the outlines of any tolerable hypothesis along these lines, because the connecting links are wanting. If it is worth while to record any personal opinion which I have been disposed to hold on the subject, it leaned in the direction of a hope that at no distant period of time more light might be forthcoming and might determine the question finally on the one or the other side. It cannot be said that I cherish such a hope now. The Hermetic literature of the seventeenth century appeared a not improbable source from which to expect assistance, and as much of it is still largely in manuscript, there remains a bare possibility that its fuller examination—e.g. at Oxford—might produce a result. But it is highly speculative, and all effort has been suspended on my own part, since the researches embodied in my *Brotherhood of the Rosy Cross* failed to produce anything that could be called tangible in this respect.

**Rosicrucian Influence**. It is therefore under more than usual reserves if I mention the views of a few writers, not altogether uninformed, according to whom the influence of the ROSICRUCIAN FRATERNITY upon that of the Masons has been questioned only by those who have been unfitted to appreciate the symbolism which they possess in common. The nature of the influence is another matter and one, moreover, in which they might be prepared to recognize the simple principle of imitation up to a certain point. They would refer it to the formative period of Emblematic Freemasonry, but for myself it belongs more especially to that of development and extension. It has been exercised obviously in connection with High Grades, as to which it is impossible—for example—to question that those who instituted the Eighteenth Degree of the SCOTTISH RITE either must have received something by transmission from the old

German Brotherhood or, alternatively, must have borrowed from its literature.

**German Views.** Outside the High Grades, there have been, moreover, writers of note and Germans are chief among them—who have regarded Freemasonry as actually a final development of the ROSICRUCIAN BROTHERHOOD. The first to advance this hypothesis was Nicolai of Berlin—a bookseller of some literary eminence—in the year 1782. He was followed by Buhle, without much otherwise in the way of agreement with the views and claims of his predecessor. Gould has ruled that the speculations of both are dead, and assuredly this is true of the specific complexion which was given them, but he himself was something more than disposed to recognize—and does in fact acknowledge implicitly—the likelihood of such a broad and gradual influence as is here under consideration. More than a century prior to the two German writers—that is to say, in the year 1638—Henry Adamson—who is described by Gould as a citizen of Perth—published a metrical account of that city in which are the following lines:

> For we are Brethren of the Rosie Cross.
> We have the Mason Word and second sight

**Elias Ashmole.** I do not know whether the significance of this quotation—which is one of the earliest references to the ROSICRUCIAN SOCIETY found in the English language—has been appreciated at its full value. It is the first occasion assuredly on which that Fraternity and Masons are bracketed, so to speak, together; in which connection it should be remembered that the earliest reports in Europe concerning Rosicrucians do not go back further than 1610. The informal relation instituted by the verses cannot be regarded as evidence, except perhaps of an implied link and bond in the mind of the writer; but even from this point of view it is not without significance. It was several years subsequently—namely, in 1651—that Rosicrucian Manifestoes were first translated into English, and it was a little prior to this time that Elias Ashmole was admitted into the Brotherhood of Masons. That he was connected previously with Rosicrucians themselves, or otherwise with the representatives of some association which had assumed their name, has been an inference drawn from his life; but it happens to be purely speculative. His antiquarian studies led him more especially in the direction of Alchemy, but as regards this art he did not remain an antiquary, a mere collector of old documents on the subject. He may not be entitled to rank as a practical student but he was much more than an unaided and isolated inquirer. He had secured that assistance which has been regarded always as next but one to essential, namely, the instruction of a Master. The alternative is Divine Aid, which is of course a higher kind of Mastery.

**William Backhouse.** The charitable instructor in the case of Ashmole was one William Backhouse, of whom few particulars are forthchoming in public beyond his asserted Rosicrucian connections. The assertion may be reducible, however, to the unquestioned fact that he followed alchemical studies—a recurring confusion of uncritical persons and times. Ashmole was associated otherwise with many of the occult philosophers, alchemists, astrologers and so forth—belonging to his period. The suggestion that he acted as an instrument of the Rosicrucian Brotherhood, or as a member thereof, in the transfiguration of Operative into Speculative Freemasonry is a matter of faith for those who have held or hold it. Of direct or indirect evidence there is not one particle. Supposing that such a design existed at the period he is not an unlikely person to have been concerned in planning it on the part of himself and others, or to have been delegated for such a purpose. But of the design there is again no evidence. The period is at most the beginning of a leavening only and not the result thereof. It has been affirmed further in the interests of the claim that a meeting of an Alchemical—presumably Rosicrucian—Order took place in London, and in a hall which was used regularly for Masonic gatherings—meaning Masons' Hall; that Ashmole and his fellow-Rosicrucians—perceiving how working Masons were already outnumbered in membership by persons of education not belonging to the trade—believed that the time was ripe for a complete ceremonial revolution and that one founded on mystical tradition was drawn up therefore in writing, constituting the ENTERED APPRENTICE Grade, approximately as it exists now. The Grade of FELLOW CRAFT was elaborated in 1648 and that of MASTER in the year 1650.

**Ashmole's Initiation.** These are the reveries of Ragon, categorical in nature, accompanied by specific details, all in the absence of one particle of fact in any record of the past. It seems to me therefore that no language would be too strong to characterize such mendacities and that they could belong only to the class of conscious lying; but the charge against Ragon is more especially that he elaborated the materials of a hypothesis which had grown up among successive inventors belonging to the type of Reghellini. If there were Rosicrucians in England at the date in question, if Backhouse was actually a Rosicrucian, it may be presumed that those who according to Ashmole's own statement communicated to him some portions at least of the Hermetic Secrets would not have withheld the corporate mysteries of their Fraternity. But on the other hand there is no historical evidence whatsoever that the Hermetic Order possessed any such corporate existence in England at that period and there is no evidence that Backhouse was himself a member—holding from abroad or otherwise. However, this may be, in the memoirs of the life of Elias Ashmole, as drawn up by himself in the form of a diary, there is the following now well-known entry under date of October 16, 1646:

I was made a Freemason at Warrington in Lancashire, with Colonel Henry Mainwaring of Kartichan in Cheshire; the names of those that were then at the Lodge: Mr Richard Penket, Warden; Mr James Collier, Mr Richard Sankey, Henry Littler, John Ellam, Richard Ellam and Hugh Brewer.

**Life of Ashmole.** The two noteworthy points in this extract, over and above the main fact which it designs to place on record, are that neither Candidate was an operative by business and that the work of initiation was performed evidently by the brother who acted as Warden. At this period Elias Ashmole was under thirty years of age. His father was a saddler by trade, his mother was the daughter of a draper and he himself solicited in Chancery. But while still in his youth he tells us that he had entered into that condition to which he had aspired always: 'That I might be able to live to myself and studies, without being forced to take pains for a livelihood in the world.' The admissions of October 16, 1646, are not required to prove the practice of initiating men of other business than that of Masonry and its connected crafts, or even of no business at all, but it should be observed that here—as in cases of earlier date—the reception was in the capacity of simple brothers and not of patrons. The practice is doubtless much older than its earliest record, and there is nothing whatever in the diary of Ashmole to indicate that the occurrence was unusual, or that he and his companion were in any sense favoured specially—as commoners who became Brethren and not as noble patrons.

**Alchemical Pursuits.** The nature of those studies which were engrossing to him about the time of his initiation may be learned by the publication, five years later, of his THEATRUM CHEMICUM BRITANNICUM, being a collection of metrical treatises written in English at various dates on the subject of the Hermetic Mystery and the Philosopher's Stone. They appear to be concerned only with what is called technically the physical work on metals and the physical medicine or elixir, not with those Spiritual Mysteries which are held to have passed occasionally into expression under the peculiar symbolism of Alchemy. At the same time Ashmole is careful to explain his personal assurance that the transmutation of metals is only one branch of Hermetic practice.

As this is but a part, so it is the least share of that blessing which may be acquired by the Philosopher's *materia*, if the full virtue thereof were known. Gold, I confess, is a delicious object, a goodly light which we admire and gaze upon *ut pueri in Junonis avem;* but as to make gold is the chief intent of the Alchemists, so was it scarcely any intent of the ancient Philosophers and the lowest use the Adepti made of this *materia*. For they, being lovers of wisdom more than worldly wealth, drove at higher and more excellent operations; and certainly he to whom the whole course of Nature lies open rejoiceth not so much that he can make gold and silver or the devils be made subject to him as that he sees the heavens open, the angels of God ascending and descending, and that his own name is fairly written in the Book of Life.

**The Hermetic Work.** I regard this extract as presenting a theory in brief of the whole Hermetic work, under the light of a peculiar extension, and it is in particular remarkable for its analogies with the books of Thomas Vaughan, a contemporary of Ashmole and about the same age. There is incorporated also a citation from the Rosicrucian *Fama Fraternitatis*. Taken altogether it suggest the opening of a certain door, beyond which there seems to stretch an endless vista, a prospect beyond prospect. It is not possible in the present place to attempt any description. It may be observed, however, by way of very brief analysis, that 'the chief intent of the alchemists' is not said to attain its term by the common way of the alchemists, being that which Vaughan calls the 'torturing of metals'. There is a certain matter which in its lowest application can produce gold but in its highest opens a path to Eternal Life. Now, we know otherwise from hermetic literature that the Stone of the Philosophers was not a stone actually, and that the Powder of Transmutation was not literally and atomically a powder. These modes of language were veils made use of by the adepts, sometimes to shew forth symbolically the higher fields of their concern, sometimes to put on record their acquaintance—hypothetical or practical—with certain renovating and transmuting substances available to operation in the lower branches of their art. It will be obvious, I may assume, that a *materia* which can be used in the making of material gold does not open the heavens, reveal the Ladder of Jacob, or enable the operator to find his name written in the Book of Life.

**Alchemical Stone**. The language of Ashmole is therefore that of parable, and a similar criticism obtains when he distinguishes elsewhere four species of so-called Philosophical Stone—mineral, vegetable, magical and angelical. Here is another allegory under which he indicates the four palmary divisions of occult science, so-called. The first is concerned with the supposed development and perfection of metallic substances; the second deals with the secret virtues of plants, about which something will be found in such books as the HERBARIUM of Paracelsus; the third is—in modern language—the science of lucidity; vision at a distance, reading in the Astral Light, and so forth; but the fourth is a celestial and divine power, by which the angelical world was supposed to be opened and by which gifts of veridic dream and prophecy were conferred upon the seer. It calls to be said that none of these Philosophical Stones opens the Book of Life, and seeing that Ashmole uses this figurative expression categorically he was aware that there is a fifth, highest and most catholic Stone—about which he does not speak—or he misconceived the way and end of research in true adeptship. I think personally that he had a very full conception and grasp of occult initiation but did not know that of the mystics, unless at a far distance and through a dark glass. However this may be, he says generally with regard to Hermetic practice:

I must confess I know enough to hold my tongue but not enough to speak, and the no less real than miraculous virtues I have found in my diligent inquiry into the arcana lead me to such degrees of admiration, they command silence and force me to lose my speech.

**Rosicrucian Doctrine.** It should be added that Ashmole's exposition is a faithful reflection of Rosicrucian doctrine as this is put forward, directly or indirectly, under the name of the Brotherhood in German books and pamphlets of the early seventeenth century. Supposing for a moment that *circa* 1650 there was a Rosicrucian School in England no person is so likely to have been a member as Ashmole, and it is not possible to imagine him in separation therefrom. Indeed I am by no means certain that his testimony would not seem thinly presumptive of membership for certain minds, being so to the manner born of it in thought and figures of speech; and they might incline to this view the more (*a*) because the literature of the Rosy Cross at the Ashmole period and earlier offers little conscious realization of the highest ends of adeptship, and (*b*) because the direction in which it falls short is that of Ashmole's own deficiency. Those who can tolerate—however tentatively—the Rosicrucian initiation of Ashmole would assuredly take it for granted that he did not stand alone. I have exhausted the Ashmole case in my work on the Rosy Cross and have found no evidence; but it is not impossible and offends against no likelihood (*a*) that on October 16, 1646, at Warrington in Lancashire, a Brother of the Rosy Cross was made a Mason, with or without an ulterior motive in view; or (*b*) that one who was already a Mason was drawn within the ranks of the German Order, secretly at work in England, some time subsequently to the Warrington episode. It follows expressly from his frank and honourable testimony concerning himself that he was one who had only seen the end of adeptship, even within the measures that he conceived it, while as regards any other Rosicrucians to whom he may have been joined we know nothing concerning them with the sole exception of Backhouse.

**The Ashmole Hypothesis.** It will be seen that the Ashmole hypothesis is but a part of the wider claim of Rosicrucian influence on the development of Emblematic Freemasonry. I have recorded and agree with the opinion that in so far as it has been advanced in the past this claim has lapsed. To put it shortly, the House of the Holy Spirit, being the ROSICRUCIAN BROTHERHOOD in Germany, had a Secret House in England which either transfigured itself into the thing called Speculative

Masonry or revolutionized the old operative Craft along speculative lines for its own purposes, presumably that it might have recruiting centres available and more or less openly manifest. With this hypothesis there lapses its earlier form, which even now is regarded favourably by a few here and there. Among the great Rosicrucian apologists of the early seventeenth century we have seen that there was the Englishman Robert Fludd, and it has been sought to connect him not only with the German Fraternity, but with the transition of Operative into Emblematic Freemasonry by an admixture of Rosicrucian doctrine and symbolism therewith.

**Robert Fludd.** Supposing that the ROSICRUCIAN SOCIETY of 1615 existed otherwise than on paper, Fludd may have been brought within it, for he had certainly wrought and fought for it throughout his literary life; but we do not know. He reflected and extended the continental Rosicrucian literature. His Masonic connections are still more slender and tentative and are reducible within two simple points of fact: (1) That he lived in his later years, as indeed he died also, in Coleman Street, close to the Masons' Hall; (2) That in the year 1660 an Inventory of the Company's goods, taken before the fire of London, has the following entry: 'Item 1, BOOK OF THE CONSTITUTIONS that Mr Flood gave'. Why it should follow that a person whose house is near Masons' Hall is likely to have been himself a Mason and why the Mr Flood mentioned in 1660 must be identified with Robertus de Fluctibus, the Kentish philosopher who died in 1637, I am not able to see; but there has been reasoning of this kind. Much has been done recently to elucidate the life and writings of the Kentish occult philosopher, but the last conclusion of his most informed biographer, the Revd J. B. Craven, is that which has been reached previously by first-hand students of his Latin works—namely, that there is no evidence of his alleged Masonic connections.

**The Operative Brotherhood.** When the question at issue has been relieved from these reveries there remains the more reasonable suggestion that the Operative Brotherhood came gradually and not unnaturally under the influence of persons who belonged to both associations. It is reasonable (*a*) because of the non-operative element within the Craft, (*b*) because this element began to predominate, (*c*) because a Craft Mystery so curiously qualified was antecedently likely to attract the members of other confraternities, having Mysteries of their own. It would attract also those who were simply Hermetic students, though isolated and unattached as such. Attached or otherwise, Ashmole is a case in point. The influence which in this manner would begin to be exercised, consciously or unconsciously, would be Hermetic in a general sense rather than Rosicrucian exclusively; but this is a distinction which will not be realized readily by those who are acquainted only at second hand with the mystical and occult movements of the seventeenth century. Finally, it may have been even older than the Commonwealth and Restoration. As to the Ritual side of the Operative Mystery in that century we know next to nothing, while of Rosicrucian Ritual procedure—if any—we know nothing at all.

**A Lost Word.** The Adamson couplet is evidence that there was a Mason's Word at the period, whereas Speculative Masonry is concerned with the Quest of a Lost Word. The distinction seems therefore generic. Granting for a moment the fact of Hermetic influence I conceive that it was gradual and indeed very slow in its working, and at *circa* 1650 we are far enough away from the invention of any Third Degree and far away from the Legend of Solomon's Temple. The latter—as it stands now—connotes a more fully developed Kabalism than belongs to the English Hermetic Schools of the date in question.

**Third Degree.** Such in rough outline is the case as it stands for the interference of Hermetic Schools in Freemasonry, prior to the first historical evidence for the Ritual of the THIRD CRAFT DEGREE and apart from any long since exploded hypothesis which has sought to connect the Brotherhood with older Mysteries, by means of direct transmission within their own bonds. After all, it is not impossible that some day it may assume a less uncertain aspect—in other words, that sources of additional knowledge may become available. But it is not worth while to exaggerate the importance of the question since that which is at issue is largely a point of date. I know that the root-matter of the THIRD DEGREE belongs to the Secret Tradition and is not only of the Hermetic Schools but of Schools thereunto antecedent. This is not a speculative question or one of simple persuasion. It is, moreover, no question of history and does not stand or fall with particular personalities and dates, and with claims made concerning them. As regards both these there may, by possibility, be work remaining to do—that is to say, in the purely historical field; but unfortunately the subject has only a few sympathizers in England, and among these a small proportion only who are qualified to work therein.

**Ragon's Reverie.** In France I have indicated that the Ashmolean hypothesis is practically an accepted explanation by those who are at the pains to seek for any: it has followed the lead of Ragon and has remained in uncritical hands, which have built up further fabrics of speculation in the guise of historical theses that cannot be called in question. Thus a late President of the Martinist Order in Paris found it possible to state with authority as certain facts: (1) That Freemasonry was established in England by members of the FRATERNITY OF THE ROSE-CROSS, who were anxious to create a centre for the protection of their Order and for recruiting purposes. (2) That the earliest Masonic Lodges were made of a composite character, in part consisting of operative craftsmen and in part of men of understanding imbued with these ulterior motives. (3) That the Rosicrucian link with Masonry began unquestionably through Ashmole. The enunciation of empirical suppositions in this language of certitude reduces an important matter of speculative research to a byword among serious students. To sum up on my own part, the Ashmolean hypothesis is a name which stands for an idea; his personal intervention in Masonry is not a matter of importance, but he represents a school, and it is the possible interference of the school in question which—in the opinion of a few—may enable us to understand better the rise and development of Emblematic Freemasonry and the existence among us of that MASTER-GRADE 'which is at once the foundation and keystone of the whole' speculative edifice.

**The Kabalistic School.** I have dealt so far with two out of the three schools; and it seems to me that their position, so far delineated, is not altogether unlike that of speculation on Comacines, Roman Collegia and Dionysian architects, except that these latter were obviously Building Guilds, while the former were symbolists, speaking a tongue of symbolism. Some of them were concerned only or chiefly with the ascent of the soul in God, some of them worked in metals, with a view of their material transmutation; but while the dedication of the former was *ab origine* spiritual that of the latter in a sense became spiritual, for such was their kind of chemistry that they claimed to behold in their alembics a reflection of the work of God in creation and the analogy of that redeeming process by which the soul is transmuted in God. They made use of these correspondences freely in their cryptic books, which deserve at their best to be termed books of devotion as well as records of physical experiments. The integration of men like these in Lodges of Masons could not fail of effect; if indeed it ever took place, except in the person of Ashmole. Our difficulty is to ascertain that there were others who followed in his steps; and this is our hindrance about the hand of Hermetic Schools in Freemasonry. When we pass, however, to a consideration of the Kabalistic or third Hermetic School the position will prove, I think, different though it may not take us further back than the eighteenth century.

**Kabalistic Tradition and Masonry..** The existence of a building secret, represented as a Master-Word, is like a pivot upon which revolves the Legend of the THIRD DEGREE. The Master-Builder died to preserve the Secret of this Word. Owing to his untimely death the Word was lost and—being unfinished at the moment of this untoward event—the Temple remained with its operations suspended, to be completed later on by those who possessed not the Grade of Knowdge represented by that Word, of which every Master Mason is hypothetically still upon the quest. What does this mean? We have no concern at the present day—except in archaology and history—with King Solomon's Temple. What is signified for us by such Temple and what is the Lost Word? The only direction in which we can look for an answer is to that which is their source. As to this it must be remembered that the Legend of the Master Grade is on the surface a Legend of Israel under the ægis of the Old Covenant, and though it has no warrant in Holy Writ it is not improbable antecedently that something to our purpose may be found elsewhere in the literature of Jewry. I do not of course mean that we shall meet with the Legend itself: it would be interesting if we did but not perhaps helpful *per se*, apart from explanation. The root-matter of much which is shadowed forth in the Legend, as regards the meaning of the Temple and the search for the Lost Word, is to be found in certain great texts known to scholars under the generic name of Kabalah—a Hebrew word meaning reception, or doctrinal teaching passed on from one to another by verbal communication. According to its own hypothesis, the tradition entered into written records during the

Christian Era, though hostile criticism has been disposed to represent it as invented at the period when it was reduced to writing. The question does not signify for our purpose, since the close of the thirteenth century is the last date that the most drastic view—now abandoned generally—has proposed for the most important text.

**Solomon's Temple.** We find therein after what manner, according to mystic Israel, Solomon's Temple was spiritualized; we find profound meanings attached to the two Pillars J and B; we find how a Word was lost and under what circumstances the chosen people were to look for its recovery. It is an expectation for Jewish Theosophy, as it is for the Craft Mason. It was lost owing to a certain untoward event, and although the time and circumstances of its recovery have been calculated in certain text, there has been something amiss with the methods. Those who were keepers of the tradition died with their faces towards Jerusalem, looking for that time; but for Jewry at large the question has passed long since from the field of view, much as the quest is continued by Masons in virtue of a ceremonial formula but cannot be said to mean anything for those who undertake and pursue it officially.

**Book of Splendour.** I am collecting things in a summary fashion that are scattered up and down the vast text with which I am dealing—that is to say, SEPHER HA ZOHAR, the Book of Splendour. The word to which reference is made is that Divine Name out of the consonants of which we have formed JEHOVAH, or—by another speculation—YAHVE. If it be asked: What is the connection between the loss and dismemberment which befell the Divine Name JEHOVAH and the Lost Word in Masonry, it is obvious that I cannot answer, except in a veiled manner; but every ROYAL ARCH Mason knows what is communicated to him in the Supreme Degree. In the light of the present explanation he will see that the 'great' and 'incomprehensible' thing so imparted comes from a Secret Tradition in Israel.

**Pillars J and B.** It is also to this Kabalistic source—rather than to the variant account in the First Book of KINGS or in CHRONICLES—that we must have recourse for light on the important Masonic Symbolism concerning the Pillars J and B. There is very little in Holy Scripture to justify a choice of these objects as particular representatives of an art of building spiritualized. But in later Kabalism, in the texts called THE

GARDEN OF POMEGRANATES and THE GATES OF LIGHT there is a very full explanation of the strength which is attributed to B, the left-hand Pillar, and of that which is 'established' in and by the right-hand Pillar, called J.

**Secret Tradition in Israel.** As regards the Temple itself I have explained elsewhere after what manner it is spiritualized in various Kabalistic and semi-Kabalistic texts, so that it appears as 'the proportion of the height, the proportion of the depth and the lateral proportion' of the created universe, and again as a part of the Transcendental Mystery of Law which is at the root of the Secret Tradition in Israel. I will say only that it offers another aspect of the fatal loss in Israel and the world which is commented on in the Tradition. That which the Temple symbolizes above all things is, however, a House of Doctrine, and as on the one hand the ZOHAR shews us how a loss and substitution were perpetuated through centuries, owing to the idolatry of Israel at the foot of Mount Horeb in the wilderness of Sinai, and illustrated by the breaking of the Tables of Stone on which the law was inscribed, so does Speculative Masonry intimate that the Holy House, which was planned and begun after one manner, was completed after another and a Word of Death was substituted for a Word of Life.

**The Word in Kabalism.** The complement in Kabalism of that Sanctuary loss to which Masonry confesses is therefore the Sacred Name, which became a dismembered symbol in Jewry. It is on record that the mode of vocalization was a Secret of the Holy of Holies and was reserved thereto. But there came upon Israel the stress and terror of that time which is called the Greater Exile, and from year to year no longer did the High Priest pass behind the veil and pronounce the Great Word on the other side of the curtain of palms and pomegranates. It came about in the course of the centuries that the true way of its pronunciation passed even from the memory of the elders. Therefore, 'until time or circumstances should restore the genuine' they continued to do of necessity that which has been done previously in accordance with the Law of the Sanctuary—by the substitution of ADONAI for JEHOVAH in the reading of the Law, and by writing the latter Name with the vowel-points of the former. 'My Name is written Jehovah but is read Adonai,' say the texts of the Holy Tradition on the part of the Master of Wisdom, and the Tradition with its whole heart looks for that day to come when Israel shall be taken out of exile and the palladium of the elect people shall be declared in the hearing of all who have come out of great tribulation into the inheritance of Zion.

**The Divine Name.**—This—as I have said—is the story on its literal side, and though it would be easy to allegorise thereon, it is of the temporal and national order. On the emblematic side it exhibits a cosmic sanction. The Divine Name is without change or shadow of vicissitude in the Supernal World; but according to tradition the HE final descended to earth at the Fall of Man as part of the scheme of His redemption, and became Shekinah in exile. The Divine Name was dismembered in this manner. But the HE final is the Bride of Messias, Who is the Divine Son, represented by the letter VAU. He is in search of His Bride through the ages. A day shall come when He also will descend to earth, that He may raise up the HE, whereby and wherein there shall be unity restored to the Name: it will be the epoch of the Great Jubilee and the Seventh Day of the Cosmos, when it shall repose in God.

**The Master-Builder.** There is no need to say that beneath such veils of allegory and amidst such illustrations of symbolism the Master-Builder will be found significant of a principle and not a person—historical or otherwise. He stands indeed for more than a single principle; and in the world of mystical intimations through which we are now moving, such a question as 'Who is the Master?' would be answered by many voices. But generally he is the imputed and very real life of the Secret Doctrine which lay behind the letter of the Written Law, which 'the stiff-necked and disobedient' of the patriarchal, sacerdotal and prophetical dispensations contrived to destroy. According to the Secret Tradition in Israel, the whole creation was established for the manifestation of this life, which unfolded actually in its dual aspects when the spiritual Eve was drawn from the side of the spiritual Adam and was placed over against him, in the condition of face to face. The intent of creation was made void in that event which is termed the Fall of Man, though this particular expression is unknown in Scripture. By the hypothesis, those 'fatal consequences' which followed would have reached their term on Mount Sinai; but the Israelites, when left to themselves in the wilderness, 'sat down to eat and rose up to play.' That which is concealed by the evasion of these last words corresponds to the state of Eve in Paradise, when she had become infected by the Serpent.

**The Greater Exile**. The Fall of Man is of course a story of Israel from the standpoint of Zoharic Kabalism, and that exile of the ages which followed the expulsion from Eden is like the exile of Jewry from Zion through the Christian centuries. When, according to the traditional dream, the elect shall come into their own it will be as if Adam went back into Paradise under the folded wings of the Cherubim, or as if the High Priest passed into the Holy of Holies. There are hence certain analogies between the literal and emblematical stories, and the loss memorized on the literal side has its complement—as I have said—in Masonry. But in all its Rites and Orders there is an analogy between the Emblematic Art and the Emblematic Myth of the Zohar. The Art recognizes after its own manner that Symbolical Masonry has one foundation and one keystone, which is the Sacred Name Jehovah, but in common with all Israel in exile it can give that Name only with the pointing of Adonai, and in so doing it is ruled out of court by the voice of the whole tradition.

**Christian Grades**. There remain, however, the Christian Grades of Masonry—as, for example, that of ROSE-CROIX, understood as a typical instance. They know nothing of Israel and its tradition of Secret Theosophy, but only that the quest of the Craft Grades is left in fine unfinished. For them and their votaries the eye is not satisfied with seeing nor is the ear filled with hearing the Divine Name, whether read and written as Jehovah or Adonai. Their hypothesis does not say that it is imperfect: it is the sum of perfection and Providence within the measures of the Old Law, but this is an unfinished experiment, and with all respect to the Masonic Grades which subsist under that obedience the Word of Quest is not to be found therein, till that which makes for completion is added thereto. Herein lies the office of the Holy and Christian Grades, and the work is done by taking the letter SHIN—which is called the letter of the Spirit—and inserting it in the Name יהוה, the result of which is יהשוה, understood as the Name of Jesus and the Word of the New Law. It will be seen therefore that the Grand Master did not come to set aside or destroy but to fulfil the Sacred Name of old, which stands about His own symbol as the hills stand about Jerusalem. He came also to fulfil the Law by the work of its transmutation from that of bondage to the Law of Grace. But the corner-stone of the New Temple was rejected by Jewry and the walls of Zion fell down. There was no Temple henceforth in Israel and no place for the chosen people. The *amplius et perfectius tabernaculum, non manu factum* rose up in the Gentile world and not in Palestine. For the Christian Grades of Masonry it was obvious therefore that the experiment of the Symbolical Degrees could be finished only in the Light and Law of Christ. In Him also the Master-Builder—whom the Craft had mourned so long—must arise if he is to restore all things.

**Christian Kabalism**. If the sources of Craft Masonry—taken at its culmination in the Sublime Degree—are thus found in Kabalism, what manner of people were those who grafted so strange a speculation and symbolism on the Operative Procedure of a Building-Guild? The answer is that all about the period which represents what is called the 'transition'—and indeed between the sixteenth and seventeenth centuries—many Latin-writing scholars of Europe were animated with zeal for an exposition of the Tradition in Israel, with the result that memorable and even great books were produced on the subject. Materials were thus provided and were ready to the hands of symbolists. What purpose had the latter in view? The answer is that in Germany, Italy, France and England the zeal for Kabalistic literature had more than a scholastic basis. It was believed that the texts of the Secret Tradition shewed plainly—out of the mouth of Israel itself—that the Messiah had come. This is the first fact. The second is in Ceremonial Masonry itself and namely, that although the central event of the Third Degree is the Candidates' Raising, it is not said in the Legend that the Master-Builder rose, thus suggesting that something remains to come after which might at once complete the Legend and conclude the Quest. The third fact is that in an important High Grade of a philosophical kind, now almost unknown, the Master-Builder of the THIRD DEGREE does actually rise as Christ—as we have found in its proper place. It follows that although the Opening and Closing of the THIRD DEGREE and the Legend of the Master-Builder, with all their speaking mystery, may seem to come from very far away, they are not so remote that we cannot trace them to their source.

**Of Spiritual Building**. If there were ever emblematic in the sense of spiritual builders, we must count the Jewish Theosophers of the greater exile as first and chief among them.

The Kabalists were builders of a city not made with hands, of a heavenly Zion, of a Temple and Sanctuary within the walls thereof, of which the Sacred House of the Eternal King in the earthly Jerusalem was but an imperfect external sign. The world for the Kabalists was full of palaces and sanctuaries, while visible creation—in particular, this lower world, the sphere of the Kingdom—was viewed as the House of Adonai, the abode of the Indwelling Glory. It will be seen how readily this conception lent itself to the institution of multitudinous analogies in the fervid mind of Jewry; how the outward Sanctuary was transfigured by many meanings, so that it was now the body of man enlightened by the abiding spirit—which was also the understanding of the Law, and now celestial Jerusalem; how the destruction—when this came about—of the material city signified the Secret Doctrine laid waste by the advocates of the letter, or again the chosen nation, the peculiar people delivered into hands of idolators; and finally, if I may plunge for a moment more deeply into the complexities of Kabalistic reverie—how the external city and its holy places were symbols of the primeval world before the serpent ascended into the Tree of Life; how the later city stands for a restored world in Kabalism, which differs from the first in glory; and how there is yet another city, which is to come, and over this a new firmament shall shine. It is this dwelling of the elect that the Kabalist rebuilds in his heart; and as I know that its splendid spectrum, like a bow of promise, rests over all the later literature of Israel, I register an inward conviction that some shadowed reflections thereof have been derived into occult associations, not even excepting Masonry from spiritual enthusiasts of the ghettos.

**The Restoration of Zion.** I know that long after the golden age of Kabalism, yet far earlier than the earliest date which we can assign to any Rituals of Initiation now worked among us, the Rosicrucian Fraternity also symbolized a sacred city and house not made with hands; while at the very period when the wonder and rumour of the ZOHAR first astonished the academies and synagogues of Spain there fell that Order of Knights Templar which speculation has always accredited with the design of restoring Zion. From this source something also has been acquired by High Grade Masonry, which has drawn from many fountains, not excepting—however indirectly—the Christian Mystics, who in their own manner dreamed of a Spiritual

Sanctuary, from the days of St Augustine and THE CITY OF GOD to those of St Teresa. The office and mission of the Church itself may be similarly regarded, for this is also a city of many palaces, which—in virtue of inherent vitality—builds itself up from within and is improved and beautified for ever by the continual transmutation of its living stones.

**Of Words made Void.** The legend of a literal Master-Word which perished with a Master-Builder—or was hidden with him in a sepulchre—which connoted rank in a sodality, or a grade of skill in craftmanship, can spell nothing whatever to us as Emblematical Masons, and from the moment that it might pass into desuetude for any reason it would lose all consequence to Operatives. Whatever substitution might be agreed upon would acquire at once the value and efficiency of the original. There would be nothing to connect, nothing to seek, for in fact there would be no loss. In certain Orders existing at this day there are Temporal Passwords which are replaced regularly by others at given times and seasons: when the old ones pass out of use they fall into the limbus of forgotten things, or are buried in the records of Minute-Books. If the Master-Word of Masonry was actually and literally a Word, then it belonged to this category, and the great quest of the Craft Degrees becomes nonsense, not only on the face of things but in their very heart. Put otherwise and more plainly, Emblematic Freemasonry is stultified at once as such. It is beyond all question therefore that either those who made it, as now practised, were dealing in another subject, which they veiled in allegory and illustrated by symbols, or that we ourselves must set thereon the seal of such an inward meaning, if in this late day of the world we are to redeem the woof of symbolism. As to its real nature I have indicated in this section the direction in which we must look. But the Secret Doctrine of Israel is another illustration by allegory and another veil of symbolism: it is of no greater profit on the merely literal and formal side that is the Legend of the Master Grade, when the sense of this is restricted within its surface aspect. When both have dissolved there emerges that Secret Doctrine which is based on experience and which tells to those who have ears—meaning those who are capable of the experience or have already passed through it—(1) that the Word is Life; (2) that this Life is Divine; (3) that it must be made flesh within us, by realization of its presence in the heart of hearts; (4) that until it has become so incarnate the Word is lost.

**Verbum Christus est**. It is to be understood that I am speaking here from the deep root of things, remembering the place of the LOGOS in philosophy and its application to the Mystery of Christ. We have to realize, however, that the symbolism of the Word in Masonry does not stand alone, but calls for consideration in connection at large with the Craft Traditional History and with that which is enacted ritually and is built up on this basis. After passing therefore through the ceremonial experience of a figurative death and resurrection, we have to recall in the first place that the Craft Masters do not find the Word which was the secret and seal of Masters in the plenary light of Masonry; they make shift for the time being with a devised and arbitrary substitute. It is as if something had been enacted symbolically which must be fulfilled hereafter in life and experience, as if the Way of Divine Life and the Way of Truth had been delineated in a metaphysical sketch and its application left to themselves in their proper persons. A quest-motive arises in this manner, and we hear of a quest in Masonry; but within the measures of the Craft Degrees it is pursued always after the same manner and reaches the same suspension. The Candidate is told, however, the direction in which he must turn if he would attain his end in Masonry. It is to that bright and Morning Star about which it is said—'whose rising brings peace and salvation' and of which we learn otherwise that this is the root and stock of Jesse, ALPHA and OMEGA, the beginning and the end, the First and the Last. It is obvious therefore that the Word in Masonry is Christ, and again that the finding of the Word is the finding also of Christ. In its preliminary meaning, the loss of the Word signifies the death of Christ. The three assassins are the world, the flesh and the devil—to make use of familiar technical and conventional terms. The Master-Builder who erected the House of Christian Doctrine is Christ Himself. From another point of view the malefactors were Pilate, Herod and Caiaphas.

**A Practical Counsel**. Amidst the high technicalities and involved reveries of the Secret Tradition in Kabalism the Doctors of later Israel remembered from time to time, and indeed continually, that which is the life of Doctrine, its realization in the heart of the student. The crown of their Theosophy in respect of the Word is contained in a single sentence which is a guarantee of experience in Israel: 'If man aspires after the Supreme and Holy Utterance'—*Verbum ineffabile*—'he draws it down from above'. It is not Jehovah or another—of the ROYAL ARCH, the *Militia Crucifera* of the TEMPLE AND HOLY SEPULCHRE, or the ROSE-CROIX, *Ordo Sanctissima*. As Mary conceived in the heart before she conceived in the body, so is the Word generated and so only is born in the heart of the Master Mason. The impregnation by which it is brought about is a seed of life; the Word becomes alive in the heart; it is an utterance found in life, a life which entered into expression. The *ne plus ultra* Grade of this Mystery had been taken by St Paul when he said: 'I live, but not I: it is Christ liveth within me'. Our verbal utterances are fore- and post-shortened, suspended and broken on our lips; they are shadows of Divine Utterance; and for want of power in speech we express only in the heart that which is the Word of Life. It is the other side of that story of secret life concerning the Temples and Palaces which we have pledged ourselves to erect for the Glory of God in the Highest: 'Most Puissant Sovereign, for want of territory we build them in our hearts'. But there comes that time for some of us when we realize in our heart of hearts that there in our hidden centre—and in the last resource there only—have we been called to the work of such building.

**The Question of Antiquity**. It is to be observed that the presence of a Kabalistic element in the Traditional History of the Craft—and elsewhere—by no means connotes antiquity; and antiquity is an impossible thing to predicate of the THIRD DEGREE, in the light of our present knowledge. By whomsoever created or developed, its author had read or heard of the Secret Tradition in Israel and drew important lights therefrom, possibly at first hand, more probably perhaps from those Latin commentaries and synopses already mentioned. The great bulk of these were compiled already if we place his work early in the eighteenth century, as we must, almost beyond doubt. Much of it was available previously, supposing that more considerable antiquity could be postulated of the THIRD DEGREE. But we must be content with what is evidentially reasonable in this respect, until time or circumstances shall provide better warrants. If we cannot get behind Desaguliers I am prepared to abide by him, who was a man of learning in his way, had read in many directions and may not have been unfamiliar with Picus de Mirandula, Riccius, Capnion, Archangelus de Burgo Nuovo and Knorr von Rosenroth. There was a time when I turned with no unhopeful eye towards the ancient Masonry of York, where it seemed colourable that many things had a hidden repository for a period; but there is nothing which comes to light. For Speculative Masonry as a whole we must rest content if we can date it no further back than the Georgian Revival period, there being no evidence that Desaguliers brought anything from Scotland except certain Grade titles. It puts an end to romantic hypotheses, but the great intimations of the THIRD DEGREE remain—a speaking pageant in symbolism, however late its origin. The Quest of the Word remains, with all Zoharic Theosophy behind it and all the Rites of Christian Masonry in front. The Craft mythos connects our Order by reflection with the chief figurative Mysteries of past ages, while the Opening and Closing of the Lodge therein are much greater than anything extant in the memorials of Greece and Egypt.

**Recurrence to Hermetic Schools**. We may therefore at this point reach a general conclusion on the Hermetic Schools and their alleged intervention for the transformation of an Operative Guild into an Emblematic Freemasonry, and it shall be expressed in such a manner as will be without detriment to ourselves or our connections as loyal and devoted Masons. In Dionysian architects, Roman Collegia, Comacines and Building Guilds of the Middle Ages I have failed to discover any traces of an art of building spiritualized. I have taken the old Gothic Constitutions and have sought to digest them like Anderson 'in a new and better method', but however they were passed and repassed through the mental alembic they have yielded nothing corresponding to 'a system of morality, veiled in allegory and illustrated by symbols'. Not even the Regius MS betrays a single vestige, though I have followed Gould anxiously. As regards the Hermetic Schools, and speaking—if I may venture to say so—as one who knows the literatures, the allegation of Albert Pike—mentioned in a previous section—is true in respect of a few world-wide symbols which prove nothing and false in all things else. There is no legend of three Grand Masters in Alchemy, there is no Substituted Word, and there is no Master of the Lodge, for there is no record of Ritual procedure among all its cloud of witnesses. The witness of Alchemy to Masonry is the witness of Elias Ashmole, the sole alchemist in the seventeenth century whom we know to have become a Mason.

The Rosicrucian influence, if granted, belongs to the spirit of things rather than to their form, for at the period in question no Ritual workings were connected with that Order: we know them only in developments, which are late in the eighteenth century and are of course beyond our scope. Provisionally and under all reserves, I am inclined to hold that it began earlier, in the sense of an atmosphere belonging to the formative period of Emblematic Freemasonry. But the great Rosicrucian maxim cited by Robert Fludd about 1630 must be ruled out unfortunately. *Transmutemini, transmutemini de lapidus mortuis in lapides vivos philosophicos* does not signify that the Brothers of the Rosy Cross had either joined or invented our figurative and speculative Art: it is rather a contrast established between material and spiritual alchemy. For the present at least, we are called also to set aside the winning speculation concerning a secret school of Emblematic Masonry coexistent through several generations or centuries with the Operative Guild and sometimes identified with Rosicrucians. There are no Rosicrucian traces prior to 1598. Moreover, the alleged school is a notion arising out of a false construction of the Regius MS.

**A Final Reduction of Issues**. We are left in this manner with the Kabalistic element, about which I have spoken plainly. But now as a last point: supposing that there is in reality no trace of the Third Degree prior to 1717; that after this epoch it was devised by a group of Masonic *literati* or alternatively by an anonymous Brother, whether famous like Desaguliers or obscure: what then is our position? My own at least is this—that the THIRD DEGREE was formulated on the basis of the Ancient Mysteries and illustrated by the lights of Kabalism—facts about which there is no open question; that it belongs as such to an old and secret tradition, though not in respect of time; that it stands on its own symbolical value; and that—in the words of Martinès de Pasqually: We must needs be content with what we have. As a student of the past, I could wish that it were otherwise; but in this as in all else the first consideration is truth. There are High Grades of Masonry for which no one in their senses predicates antiquity, and yet they are great Grades. They are even holy Grades, which—from my point of view—carry on the work of the Craft toward something that stands for completion. I conclude, therefore, with an affirmation which I have made in other places, that antiquity *per se* is not a test of value. I can imagine a Rite created at this day which would be much greater and more eloquent in symbolism than anything that we work and love under the name of Masonry. Yet for what Masonic antiquity is—let us call it two hundred years and over, under all needful reserves—such an invention would not have the hallowed and beloved associations which have grown about our Emblematic Craft. Here is the matter of antiquity which really signifies: it is part of the life of the Order. And after all the fables and all the fond reveries, the false analogies and mythical identifications with other and immemorial Mysteries, it is again the life which counts, the life of that great world-wide Masonic organism, in which we ourselves live and move and have our Masonic being.

# 5
# THE ROYAL AND MASONIC ART

In 1921 Waite acquired a remarkable collection of eighteenth-century French manuscripts of masonic rituals, which he described as 'a mirror of Masonry in all its schools and development'. For him the importance of the collection lay in the support the more obscure rituals gave to his thesis of a Secret Tradition within Freemasonry, and he utilized them to that end in his later studies of the 'High Grades' (as he termed what are now known as 'additional degrees'). But Waite also recognized that from both an historical and textual point of view the manuscripts would be of great interest to all masonic scholars, and he prepared *The Royal and Masonic Art* as a general, introductory account of his *Collection Maçonnique*. The paper was first read to the Northumbrian Masters' Lodge in November, 1925, and later (October 1927) printed in the American journal, *The Master Mason*.

BEHIND the familiar world of Craft rituals, their extension in the Mark and Arch and all that is superposed upon them under the denomination of High Grades, there lies an obscure region of research which has great attractions for the specialist, but can be only imperfectly explored. It is that of their original, or at least their early, forms.

The difficulty would be peculiar in any case, since it is obvious that without the guiding spirit of discerning care and skill no real record could be obtained, as silence imposes itself on those who belong to a secret Order. The counsel of caution is addressed, however, to intelligence, and those who are qualified to follow a quest in ritual are acquainted with the limits over which they must not pass, and do not fail to deal in a due and lawful way with materials which come into their hands. The difficulty under notice has been called peculiar for this reason, yet it is not of itself inhibiting. But there is a second in the same category, and unfortunately it suspends research; the materials themselves are wanting. There is no one among us who can claim to have seen authentic early copies of the Craft rituals, and how much less their originals, as they first came into the hands of Masters and Wardens under the obedience of the Grand Lodge, *post* 1717.

The absence of authentic materials has led some students to search surreptitious publications of the eighteenth century for traces of actual procedure behind the doors of lodges in the days to which they belong. Indeed, it is admitted tacitly that such works are comparable more probably to emporiums of stolen goods rather than mere inventions. I have inclined to another path of inquiry, actuated by the very obvious fact that when Masonry passed over to the continent of Europe, that which it carried was the original Craft rituals, whatever they were.

An investigation like this is again beset with some serious surface difficulties, for it can be pursued only on the continent, except casually, and the most fruitful of all places is likely to be France, where the Craft took root both early and deeply, not to speak of the strange growths which were grafted there on the Masonic tree. Now the place of the records, if any, is in the archives of the Grand Orient and Grand Lodge of France, but, for reasons which are known to all, we are not in communion with those bodies, since they have ceased to be Masonic for us. So, also, the Supreme Council of England and Wales, which governs the Scottish or Ancient and Accepted Rite, holds no communication with the French Supreme Council. Their resources are sealed in this manner, for we cannot approach them as Masons.

It may happen, however, that the spark of unexpected opportunity will fall, so to speak, from heaven, as it has done in my own case, though it has by no means presented me and is unlikely to provide anyone with a French version of emblematic degrees as they were worked in France prior to 1750. If Great Britain, which is the source and origin of emblematic Freemasonry, can produce, so far, nothing of this kind for our instruction, there is no antecedent likelihood that we can fare better abroad, were it possible to pursue an exhaustive and expert inquiry through all the scattered directions. I will leave things of very late or dubious date which have passed through my hands, and some of which I have been enabled to translate from the originals in their MS form; they include catechisms which do not correspond to our lectures, unless at a far distance, form, of course, excepted. These are in the past of a quest which has been followed for a long time; but it is to be counted a memorable epoch when there came into my possession twelve beautiful volumes in a clear French hand, written on rag paper, prior to the French Revolution and bearing as a watermark the Royal Arms of France.

The volumes are entitled *Collection Maçonnique* and contain over seventy complete rituals extending to three thousand and more pages. Many of the items are utterly unknown in England, while in the case of some which are familiar to Masonic students, by name or otherwise, they present variations and extensions which constitute distinct texts or codices. It should be understood that the twelve volumes do not answer to the contents of a particular colossal Rite like that of Memphis or that again of Mizraim. They are the work of a private collector who followed a certain order and probably devoted several years to his task. But it happens, fortunately, that the earliest and most important, historically, of French Rites established on a considerable scale is found almost complete in the series.

Speaking of the collection as a whole, I am acquainted at a distance with one set of archives in their likeness, and this is in a catalogue of MSS belonging to the Grand Orient of the Netherlands. The set is contained in nine volumes, which correspond—with a negligible variation of arrangement—to my own series, vols. 2 to 8 and vol. 12, under the general title of Royal and Masonic Art, which I have borrowed, therefore, for obvious resons as a designation for this study. Moreover, the title at its value answers much better to my *Collection Maçonnique* than to that of The Hague, from which the Craft Degrees are missing, not to speak of an adoptive Rite, an extensive history of Masonry linked up with a procedure in ritual, and a sequence of mystic degrees.

In a word, all classes are represented in my volumes. Ecossais and Elect Grades, Grades of Chivalry, an elaborate development of Rose Croix Masonry, ceremonial reflections of magical and occult arts and remarkable presentations of the Secret Tradition in Freemasonry. Though possibly undesigned by the unknown editor, the series as a whole reflects the evolution of the Masonic subject in France being the font and source of the

High Grade movement. The twelve volumes stand, therefore, for something approaching a thousand rituals which are known to German and French bibliographers. Their contents were collected subsequently into the Scottish Rite, the Rites of Memphis and Mizraim and several smaller systems. They fall naturally into certain classes, and under such heads it is my intention to speak of them briefly.

A word, therefore, in the first place, concerning the Rite of Perfection, which I have shown elsewhere to have been founded in Paris in or about the year 1758. It was either from the beginning or became subsequently, by a process of development, an extensive numerical scheme of ritual in the form of a series, extending in all to 25 degrees, it being understood that the first three were those of the Craft. Their original general denomination is uncertain, that which I have given being of more general use and wont. It was alternatively the Rite of Heredom, otherwise a Council of the Emperors of the East and West, these exalted personalities being also Sovereign Prince Masons, Substitutes General of the Royal Art—whatever this may have been held to mean—and Grand Surveillants and Officers of the Grand Sovereign Lodge of Jerusalem, recalling that Grand Royal Arch Chapter of Jerusalem, the hypothesis in dream of which is so well known among us.

That which seems to me the most important point of my collection is, that it contains not only 21 grades belonging to the Rite of Perfection, but the first 14 appear seriatim, occupying the first three volumes. An intervention of Ecossais Grades breaks the sequence in the fourth, some of the remaining items being scattered through the next three. It is speculatively possible that apparently missing numbers are represented under other titles, for these things were always changing.

The unbroken series is as follows: (1) Apprentice Mason; (2) Lodge of Companion; (3) Lodge of Master; (4) Secret Master; (5) Perfect Master; (6) Intimate Secretary, called also English Master and Master by Curiosity; (7) Intendant of the Buildings, otherwise Little Architect; (8) Provost and Judge, or Illustrious Irish Master; (9) Elect of Nine; (10) Elect of Fifteen; (11) Sublime Elect, or Sublime Elect Knight of Justice, which is important for the traditional perpetuation of Masonry through the centuries and onward to Christian Times; (12) Grand Architect, or Grand Master Architect, in which the Holy

Shekinah is represented as delivering oracles between the wings of the cherubim; (13) Royal arch of Enoch, otherwise Knight of the Royal Arch; (14) Grand Elect Perfect Master and Sublime Ecossais, described as the last Grade of Ancient Masonry and occupying an entire volume of the *Collection Maçonnique*, in all 265 pages.

In the Scottish or Ancient and Accepted Rite, which incorporated and extended the Rite of Perfection, this epoch-making degree as known in England is called Scotch Knight of Perfection, but the recension is truncated and a mere shadow of the original, while the version of Albert Pike in his colossal transformation of the whole sequence for the use of the Southern Jurisdiction, U. S. A., is out of all relation thereto, as the true codex had not come into his hands. I am probably its only possessor in English-speaking countries.

With regard to the scattered rituals found in the rest of the volumes, they seem to have been placed by their transcriber in accordance with a rough sequence devised by himself. This accounts for the Ecossais Grades, which, as I have said, are in the fourth volume, following on the Elect Grades. When the Rite of Perfection proceeded from matters belonging to the old alliance and opened Masonic considerations referable to the Christian era, he thought it logical—outside this Rite—that a chivalry of the Holy Sepulchre should precede anything else, and it is followed by Grades of Templar Knighthood. It is to be feared that the good intention passed too soon into complete confusion, but—as so often happens in grade Masonic rituals—the grades are themselves confused, and things belonging to the symbolical time of the old covenant are represented symbolically in a lodge or chapter which obviously belongs to the new. One is liable to travel from Babylon, bearing the name of Zerubbabel, and to be pledged in the faith of the Holy Trinity, while twelve lights or other emblems may represent not only the Tribes of Israel, but the Apostles of our Lord.

The scattered rituals belonging to the Rite are (1) Knight of the East, called otherwise Knight of the Sword in the Ancient and Accepted Series; (2) Prince of Jerusalem; (3) Knight of the West—alternately, of the East and West; (4) Sovereign Prince of Rose Croix of Heredom, called also the Eminent Order of the Knights of the Black Eagle, extending to 200 pages and claiming to be the true end of Masonry. In consonance with our own attributions it is described further as a Knighthood of the Pelican and Eagle; (5) Noachite or Prussian Knight; (6) Knight of the Sun, of which, however, this is a second and larger version, or, more correctly, a totally distinct grade, being Grand Ecossais of the Crusades, Patriarch of the Great Light and Knight of the Sun; (7) Grand Inspector of Kadosh, unquestionably the primitive and far simplest form of this celebrated degree. The missing numbers are (1) Grand Pontiff or Master *ad vitam;* (2) Grand Master of the Key of Masonry; (3) Prince of Libanus; (4) Sovereign Prince of Masonry, otherwise Grand Knight and Sublime Commander of the Royal Secret. It may be thought that all these magnificent titles, unheard-of ranks and prerogatives were the satirical commentary of French High Grade Masonry on the suppositious equality of the Craft degrees.

Having given a considerable enumeration, the next point must seek to establish its purpose; and in the first place it is evident that the *Collection Maçonnique* is the work of an intelligent transcriber, but nothing more. He had access, let us say, to a common prototype of his own and the Dutch copyist, or, if the latter derived from him, he drew on his own part from some kind of archives in keeping at some Masonic centre. It comprises the Rite of Perfection in an unbroken series up to and including the Fourteenth Degree and some others of its content in a piecemeal fashion, with much further material of which I shall speak presently. There is not the least reason to suppose that he altered anything, in which case it does not seem improbable that we have the Rituals of Heredom more or less as they came forth from the mint or factory of the Emperors and their Rite of Perfection; but this system belongs, as we have seen, to the year 1758 or its immediate neighbourhood with a limit, on the further side, of 1754, which has been suggested once or twice in the past.

With these dates we may contrast the first unquestionable evidence of Freemasonry established in France, namely, the *Freemason's Pocket Companion* of 1736, according to which we know that there was a lodge then at work in *La Rue des Boucheries*, Paris and that it had been constituted on April 3, 1732. I have no brief for maintaining that there was nothing earlier, but it lies within a great cloud of fable and indubitable romance. The year 1732 is of consequence, for a very different reason than the story of a Freemasonry in France, for there is evidence that under this date Lodge No. 85 was working three degrees. We hear of them also in Prichard's *Masonry Dissected* of 1730, if we regard that publication as containing evidential matter. Between this date and the year 1717 there is no documentary ground for supposing that the new Grand Lodge had any ritual procedure in their hands but that which was brought over from the operative past. After long consideration, I have reached the conclusion, which had been reached also by many others, and have registered it elsewhere, namely, that the three emblematical and symbolical degrees of 'pure and ancient Freemasonry' were in the making between 1723 and *circa* 1730.

Under these circumstances it seems to me that the content of French Craft rituals in the year 1758 are of great importance, and I proceed in the second place to the consideration of these which were incorporated in or about that date by the Rite of Perfection, as represented by my *Collection Maçonnique*. My tentative assumption that they have not been altered from the original forms of the Rite will be remembered in this connection. It is put forward under every reserve, as ordinary caution directs, not to speak of what experience has taught me about the fallibility of expert criticism and expert speculation. We shall see in a moment, however, what is to be said on the date of my transcripts, though I do not know that any grave question attaches to this point, as they depend obviously from anterior documents, some of which may be later than others, having regard to the mass of material outside the Rite of Perfection contained within the volumes.

If we think for a moment of Scottish and Irish workings, of those which prevail in England under the name of Emulation, Stability, Oxford, Emblematic, East End, and so forth, it may seem to us that French Craft rituals about the middle of the eighteenth century will have differences greater than is exhibited by and between these; but we shall not be prepared for their magnitude, within and without the discovery which will be made at the very beginning.

More especially in the Craft degrees, but speaking generally throughout, the characteristics of French Freemasonry in these comparatively early days was to make short work of procedure in the business of opening and closing. It was essential to ascertain that the proper symbolical hour had been reached in the former case, and this determined, the lodge was declared open. It was closed in the same manner, the one variation being in respect of the time, and as this was understood tacitly, the prevailing formula in the bulk of manuscript rituals affirms only that 'the lodge is closed as it was opened'. We shall realize the force of this distinction by remembering what takes place between ourselves in a Lodge of Masters, and one is disposed to speculate whether our suggestive and indeed pregnant forms of opening and closing in the Third Degree, leaving out all that appeals to us in the First and Second, could have been in existence when the Craft first went over to France. It is difficult to believe that symbolism so important would have been omitted of set purpose. There should be mentioned in this connection the fact that my collection is subsequent to 1761, as one of its Rites is said to have been established during this year at Marseilles. I am inclined to place it tentatively between 1780 and 1785, in which case another point arises. The Craft degrees which open my first volume may represent adaptations devised for the purpose of a particular Rite, that of Perfection, for example, otherwise the Emperors of the East and West; but there will be occasion to look back on this question at a later stage.

In the degree of Entered Apprentice the candidate who seeks to be made a Mason is taken into a cabinet where an officer known as Brother Terrible raises a dagger against him and is restrained with difficulty by the expert brother who is acting as Guide. A considerable discourse follows concerning the qualifications required in postulants for Masonry—a pure heart, love of virtue, constant practise of goodness, the sacrifice of one's own will, and so forth, the virtues of secrecy being of course included. When assurance has been given in these and all other respects, the preparation of the candidate proceeds and he is at length brought into the lodge, after several checks and hindrances, again to be searched and questioned, for he has entered a House of Sacred Mysteries, which is also a place of peace. He is taken on strange journeys, is made to believe that he has entered a vault where lie the bones of traitors, is caused to drink a cup of bitterness and consents even to the shedding of his blood, though this trial is spared him. He is, in fine, pledged, but the obligation unfortunately is not committed to writing. He is sealed with the seal of the Order, after which he is admitted and proclaimed. I have passed over certain points which recall our own procedure; but they are few and far between, except in modes of preparation and in official secrets. There are others in a catechism which follows, and it transpires therein that the candidate was pledged on the New Testament, an important point, which may be compared with the demand for his baptismal name when he stands on the threshold of the lodge.

In the degree of Companion, which corresponds to that of Fellow-Craft, he is seeking to become acquainted with the mysteries of the letter G and is called upon to testify concerning his purpose in the capacity of an Entered Apprentice. As if one who should know already the high purpose of the Order, he is asked who set him to his work and to whom will he look for wages. He answers as he can, for there is no official form, and it may well be wide of the mark. He might reply with the great mystics that he came forth from the centre and would receive his recompense when he was drawn back therein, or to that point from which it is said among us that the Mason cannot err. He might say, alternatively, that his work was to seek out God. Who recompenses those who do so, for their wages are the finding of God.

But in the literal side at least the grade itself was not acquainted with these high matters, as the Master proceeds to explain. It comes about in this manner—and for us out of due season—that the Companion hears of King Solomon's Temple, when it is in the course of erection, of the Apprentices employed on the northern side, of the Master who ruled and paid them, and of the name by which he was known. There is also an explanation of hidden meanings contained in the procedure, symbolism and official secrets of the First Degree. For example, the hoodwink signified the cloud over the mind of the candidate respecting the mysteries of Masonry, while the obstacles placed in his path throughout the various circumambulations represent the difficulties which must be surmounted in the course of their earthly pilgrimage by those who would attain the Lodge in Heaven. The candidate learns further that Fellow-Crafts or Companions performed their work on the southern side of the Temple and there obtained their dues.

It is less easy to speak of procedure in the Master Grade, because for the first time we are confronted with points of correspondence between modern workings and those of the French Rite. But points of distinction are notable, and there may be observed among others: (1) The congregation of all present about the lodge in attitudes of grief and desolation; (2) the very curious position assumed by one of the Master Masons in connection with the symbolical arrangements of the centre; (3) the rough treatment of the candidate on his entrance into the lodge, he being seized violently and so brought to his place; (4) the lighting of candles of the dead at a certain stage of the proceedings, after the manner of the Roman church; (5) the details preceding the raising; (6) the blood-stained veil which covers the face of the candidate.

In a catechism which follows the active part of the ceremony it is said that Master Masons are engaged in erecting the tomb of the Master Builder, not as in a certain great Grade of St Andrew, where they are more properly awaiting his resurrection and have repaired thereto. We hear also that a certain symbolical journey from East to West is not on the quest which we follow, but in order to spread the light, and that the proof in chief of a Master Mason is that he knows the Acacia. It remains to be said that the traditional history of the Third Degree exhibits many variations from the forms extant among us, but they offer nothing of importance until towards the end, where there is an important difference as to the origin of the official secrets, while the story closes without reciting the capture and punishment of the murderers.

The last point leads us to the next and third stage of our inquiry and gives us at the same time a certain key of criticism. The Craft degrees incorporated by the Rite of Perfection were introductions only to a great scheme of ritual, the particulars of which are before us; there were Greater Mysteries to follow those which were presumably held as Lesser; and as it is not to be assumed that they were the work of a single mind, but were the creation of several anonymi; being drawn from here and there, we do not find a logical sequence which obtains throughout.

It is not an ordered Rite unfolding from small beginnings to greater ends, and yet there is a certain crude intent that prevails throughout, an endeavour to trace that Secret Tradition which is called the Royal Art in all its migrations, from a postulated beginning in immemorial times, the Christian centuries, the age of chivalry and thence onward to emblematic Freemasonry of the eighteenth century.

With such a purpose in view we can understand that the Rite, or rather its unknown makers, would modify at need the Craft rituals and thus insure their harmony with the broad design. But it happens that there was one direction only in which their scheme demanded a specific omission, on the hypothesis that the traditional history of the Third Degree stood as it stands now among us; these were the episodes of the pursuit, discovery and punishment of the three evil craftsmen who destroyed the Master Builder. The reason was that the Master Grade was to be followed by others which dealt with these subjects, namely the Elect Grades, so denominated because Solomon elected, chose or appointed certain brethren to undertake the quest involved by the demands of justice. They were Craftsmen according to our traditional history, but Masters in the Rite of Perfection, for the purely logical reason that it is the candidate who apprehends the murderers in the Elect Grades, and he is already a Master Mason.

Having discovered in this manner that which the Rite of Perfection was bound to alter in view of its later content, how are we to account for the vast differences between the French Craft degrees as here summarized and those which comprise for us the scheme of emblematic Freemasonry? Our French brethren of the eighteenth century were keen symbolists, as the inevitable catechism which follows every grade shows throughout these twelve volumes. Had they been acquainted therewith, it is not to be supposed, as we have seen, that they would have excluded the eloquent and pregnant quest for the Word in the opening and closing of the lodge according to the Master Grade. It is the typical Quest of Masonry, out of which the Symbolical Craft itself arises and on which the true High Grades depend as much as the Craft and Arch.

But they were equally keen moralists and never missed an opportunity to enforce an ethical lesson. From this point of view it would be difficult to think of anything that would have appealed to them more strongly than our moral explanations of working tools in all the three degrees. But the tools are not explained, nor are they ever exhibited. The Second Degree's invitation to study the mysteries of nature and science may sound rather hollow to us in these days, and a quick-witted candidate might confuse a Master subsequently be demanding in which of a thousand branches he himself has specialized; but in those Voltairean times I cannot help thinking that it would have enchanted French Freemasons, and probably they would have enlarged thereon.

There is, however, no word about it; and it comes to me with considerable force that when Craft Masonry first went over to France it carried something very different in ritual to that which is known among us, while the earlier we can trace the travellings the more different it is likely to have been. There is something to be said for the thesis outside the irresistible conclusions from ritual confronted with ritual. Those who have attempted to trace the sporadic history of the Mark and Royal Arch, the unaccountable genesis of the Royal Order of Scotland somewhere in southern England, and the apparition, north and south of the Tweed, of High Grades which did not come from France, will know that Great Britain—not to speak of Ireland—was a factory of grades and rituals under the Masonic ægis in the second half of the eighteenth century. Of such rituals there were made codices, and some of them differ among themselves not less conspicuously than the French differ from English Craft degrees. On these grounds only, it seems to me more certain than probable that the rituals of Entered Apprentice, Fellow-Craft and Master Mason, as worked now among us, grew up to what they are by successive rectifications and revisions from a comparatively simple and primitive root-matter, of which the French rituals under consideration here may offer no inexact notion.

I have left little space to look at the other classes of Masonic developments in France, represented by my collection of Grades. There is, firstly, all that belongs to the Sacred Word in the hiddenness, the circumstances under which it was revealed and its transmission through the ages. The beginnings of this curious *theosophia* are in Elect Knight of Twelve, which postulates Masonic Confraternity perpetuated from the days of Solomon and the completion of the First Temple. It is carried a short distance further in Knight of the Royal Arch, which becomes that of Enoch in later codices; and it reaches plenary development in the Grand Elect Grade. A side issue, so to speak, will be found in that of Noachite, which accounts for the Secret Tradition being found in Germany, while Grand Patriarch of the Crusades offers an alternative review of the whole subject at great length.

We know that the tradition is invented and that nothing in reality descended, yet is there some air of sincerity about the externalized dream. I do not doubt that it was the work of people who thought that the Lost Word of Masonry was a real and great portent, that strange things lay behind it and that it was old as the immemorial hills, because of all that they heard concerning it in rumours of Jewish Kabalism. Of Kabalism itself they knew nothing, so they went to work on the Word and its history, half believing, maybe, that they were getting at the truth of the myth when they were only making it up. In any case the Secret Tradition in Freemasonry is a very curious broth brewed in the kitchens of free speculation through a period of some fifty years.

The Ecossais Grades, of which there are some seven examples, are also curious in their way and are designed to show that Freemasonry was, so to speak, Christian, in and before Christ. The Ecossais branch descends from St John the Baptist, who founded it on the banks of the Jordan. It aims at establishing a new Masonry in the likeness of Salem the Blessed, coming down four-square out of heaven, and remembers that the Lodge of the Universe is governed by the Holy Trinity, but also the *Loge Ecossais;* it opens in the light of God and so also closes.

The candidate professes apostolic Christianity, which in that time and place would signify the faith of Rome, and we shall understand therefore what is meant when one of the obligations pledges him to serve the true God. It should be understood that I am speaking in summary form and gleaning from several grades. There is even an office in Bread and Wine, with a spiritual understanding concerning it, after which a sword is presented to defend 'our Holy religion'. It would appear that Ecossais Masonry was for the maintenance of the Latin Church and the increase of devotion thereto within the bosom of the Order.

The Grades of Chivalry which fill the later volumes are also militantly Christian and they raise the whole question of Templar-Masonic connections, with which I have dealt fully on other occasions. They can be mentioned here only to show that the *Collection Maçonnique* is indeed a mirror of Masonry in all its schools and developments. The great Rose Croix Chivalry of Heredom—which of course is not Templar—is represented by an elaborate ritual of 200 pages, divided into two parts or sections, in the first of which there is a blend of Hermetic and psuedo-Kabalistic reverie, accompanied by curious sigils, recalling those in some of the magical *grimoires*. The second portion is that only which offers analogies with the 18th Degree, as this is known among us under the obedience of the Ancient and Accepted Rite, and it is of historical consequence as an early form thereof. There is no connection whatever with the first part.

The last thing which calls to be mentioned in this long sequence is a mystical rite in three degrees under the Craft titles; but I have given some account of their translation in a critical monograph, with illustrations from the writings of psuedo-Dionysius and Heywood's *Hierarchy of the Blessed Angels*.

In conclusion, the claim made at the beginning seems to be justified at the end. The twelve manuscript volumes which came into my hands some three or four years ago are representative of Masonry in all its branches—the Craft or Symbolical Rite, Ecossais and Elect Degrees, Grades of the Secret Tradition and the Christology of the Secret Tradition, Templar and other Orders of Chivalry, even so-called mystical or rather occult grades, with one example drawn from the cryptic symbolism of alchemical quest. There is one thing wanting only and that is any trace of the Mark; it was never heard of in France in the eighteenth century and is not heard of now.

# 6
# A LODGE OF MAGIC

In 1884 the French occultist Papus (Gérard Encausse) founded the Martinist Order at Paris, and Waite joined its English branch in 1897—four years before his initiation into Freemasonry. By 1903, however, his Martinist activities had virtually ceased, which is not as surprising as it may seem, for Waite's enthusiasm was for the ideas of Louis Claude de Saint-Martin and not for the rituals which bore his name. Waite knew that Saint-Martin instituted no rituals, and that those associated with his name stemmed ultimately from his mentor, Martinès de Pasqually, whose *Rite des Élus Cohens* is the subject of this essay. But *A Lodge of Magic* does more than provide a sidelight on one of the most obscure quasi-masonic Orders of the eighteenth century; it also illustrates Waite's absolute conviction of the supremacy of mysticism over magic. The essay was first printed in *The Occult Review*, Volume 26, No. 6, for December 1917.

THERE was a period in the latter part of the eighteenth century, and more especially in France, when the evolution of High Grade Masonry embraced within the circle of its concern the chief branches of occult science. Rites were established in which the symbolism and procedure of Alchemy were illustrated and explained, while more than one among these laid claim to a peculiar knowledge concerning the mystery. For the most part, however, they were instituted to incorporate persons having a common interest and to place at the disposal of Lodge, Chapter, or Conclave whatever individual discoveries might be made from time to time. So also there were Grades for those who were disposed to the study of Astrology, and systems were devised to elucidate, under the pretence of Masonry, sometimes in a practical manner, the phenomena of Animal Magnetism, Somnambulism and Clairvoyance. The so-called Egyptian Rite of Cagliostro bore this complexion, though it had other and wider aims. It is now generally known that a lucid or clairvoyant—a young boy or maiden—was employed in one of the Degrees to obtain visions in the crystal and to pronounce oracles. Finally there were Grades which belonged in one sense or another to the multifarious concern of Magic. Most of these inventions were of an exceedingly puerile kind, and speaking on the basis of research into their now obscure byways, it is difficult to understand how they were tolerated even for a moment, above all in Paris—perhaps in that day the most enlightened city of Europe.

But though this criticism is of wide application it must not be supposed that it obtains everywhere. As the great hosts of High Grades, or things superposed on the original Craft of Symbolical Masonry, are for the most part negligible, and in the majority even worthless, but a few items stand out as stars in the emblematic firmament, and are not for an age but for all time in Ritual, so in the particular sections which belong to the occult order there is one Rite which emerges, at once peculiar in its claims and important in respect of its brief history, because of the personalities connected with it. This was the Rite of Elect Priests,* which appears to have had a Sovereign Tribunal at Paris in the year 1767, at the head of which was that mysterious, magnetic personality, Don Martinès de Pasqually. He himself is first heard of at Toulouse in the year 1760, furnished with a hieroglyphical charter and the title of Inspector-General. About 1762 he proceeded to Bordeaux, where he instructed certain brethren and laid apparently the real foundations of his Rite.

To what extent he may have been the actual creator of his own Grades and their Rituals must be left an open question in the present state of our knowledge. That they do not come before us, so to speak, ready made, like Minerva from the brain of Jupiter, is shown by the fact that in the autumn of 1768 he

---

* *Le Rite des Élus Cohens*, the last word being corrupt Hebrew, as it is supplied with a French plural. The number of Grades varies in different accounts, but they were probably ten, of which the last was a variant of Rose Croix Masonry, or otherwise of the old Rosy Cross presented in Ritual form.

was working towards their completion, seemingly amongst many distractions.* That in their root-matter they were not of his own invention would follow from a single statement made by himself† and depends, therefore, on his own sincerity, in which I register my personal belief—at whatever value may attach to it. He testified as follows on the occasion in question: 'I have never sought to lead any one into error or otherwise deceive those who have come to me in good faith, that they might share in certain knowledge which has been handed down to me by my predecessors'. It has been suggested that those predecessors were Brethren of the Rosy Cross,‡ which is by no means impossible, having regard to Rosicrucian activities at and about that time, but evidence is wanting on the point.

As I am not writing a chapter of Masonic history from a Masonic point of view, the question of origin may be left at this stage. The Rite itself, as we know it, made use to a certain extent of Masonic symbolism, subject to a particular unfolding of its inward spiritual meaning. In the latter respect it differs from Masonry, more especially in the Craft and its immediate dependencies, where interpretation does not extend beyond the simple matter of ethics. While the apprentice of the great Emblematic Order is instructed to act always as a moral man and a brother, the apprentice, or rather the novice, of the Elect Priesthood was—at least by the hypothesis—taught (*a*) the knowledge of the Great Architect, (*b*) the spiritual emanation of man from the Divine Centre, and (*c*) his direct correspondence with his Master.

The distinction thus established leads to another which is neither of symbolism nor instruction of the intellectual kind. It separates as such the Rite of Elect Priests from anything that is called Masonry in the recognized acceptance of this term. Masonry is circumscribed always within measures of symbolism,

---

* See the letter of Pasqually to J. B. Willermoz, dated September 2 1768, and quoted by Papus in his monograph entitled *Martines de Pasqually*, 1895, pp. 32, 33.

† See *Ibid.*, Letter of April 13, 1768, p. 122.

‡ *Ibid*, p. 150.

figurative procedure and emblematic ritual hereunto belonging. Pasqually came forward under warrants of another kind. As a man of interpretation he was unquestionably in the chain of the mystics, but in his practical work he was a Magus, and his Rite was a Magical Rite. However much it may have been 'veiled in allegory and illustrated by symbols', so far as liturgies are concerned, behind all this there lay—by the hypothesis concerning it and actually on the faith of the records—a very remarkable form of occult procedure. It may have taken place only in the inner circles, that is to say, in the highest Grades of the Order, but there were certain ceremonial workings which, according to the available evidence, produced actual results. It differed considerably in method as well as utterly by intention from the extant processes and formulæ of the thing called Practical Magic, yet it had sufficient analogies with this to show, whence it was in part at least derived. It is possible indeed to identify the actual sources up to a certain point. They are not of our concern here. The purpose in view was not one of communication with either good or evil spirits belonging to the dubious hierarchies of occult literature and undertaken for the trumpery if not evil concerns with which we are all acquainted, by the repute of Grimoires and so called Keys of Solomon. It was, according to one of its descriptions, 'the acquisition—by bodily, psychic and spiritual purity—of powers which enable man to establish relations with invisible beings, called angels by the churches, and to attain thereby not only the operator's personal reintegration'—or restoration of the bond of living union between the human and Divine—'but also that of all his disciples who are persons of goodwill'.*

It was more, however, than this, and was actually to manifest within the circle of assembly a Being, who is described in a veiled manner as the 'Unknown Agent charged with the work of Initiation' and 'the Unknown Philosopher', but is unquestionably understood to have been a manifestation of the Christ of Nazareth. The depositions affirm, moreover, that He came as a teacher among the Brethren, and—if we may judge by the literary remains of Pasqually, as a reflection of the things so received—that which He taught was a hidden meaning and

---

* See Papus: *Martinésisme, Willermosisme, Martinisme et Franc-Maçonnerie*, 1899, p. 7.

wisdom behind the letter of Christian doctrine.* The instruction was reduced into writing, for it is said that 'the Agent dictated',† and in this manner it became available for a period within the sanctuary of the Rite—presumably the centre at Lyons. It has been said that a part of the record was subsequently incorporated by Louis Claude de Saint-Martin into his first work entitled *Des Erreurs et de la Vérité*.‡ I do not believe this in any literal sense, but—on the assumption that we are dealing throughout with genuine archives of the Order—it is not beyond possibility that something was reflected into the work just mentioned, for Saint-Martin belonged to the circle in his earlier days, and we must remember that he wrote usually under the pseudonym of the 'Unknown Philosopher'. He testified, moreover, to his certitude (*a*) that a great power was manifested in the presence of Pasqually; (*b*) that it was the power of the 'Repairer' or Christ; and (*c*) that there was every token furthermore not only of the Christ-Presence, in the sense of the Divine Man of Nazareth, but also of the Divine Word.§ This is very high testimony on the part of an honourable and distinguished witness, who is unimpeachable on the score of good faith, whether or not it may be possible to accept his verdict as to the actual source of communication. The evidence otherwise rests upon certain archives which came—it is thirty years since—into the possession of the Supreme Council of the Order of Martinism. There is no question as to their general authenticity, and a mass of similar material is also in private hands. So far as it has been made public we are indeed indebted to the zeal of the late Dr Papus, who was President of that Order. He was not, unfortunately, a man of critical mind, and he was not to be trusted as a safe guide on matters of research or on inferences drawn from facts. Independent writers in France,

---

\* See Martinès de Pasqually: *Traité de la Réintégration des Êtres*, Bibliothèque Rosicrucienne, 1899; and Franz von Baader: *Les Enseignements Secrets de Martines de Pasqually*, 1900.

† Papus: *Op. cit.*,        ‡ Papus *Ibid.*, p.14.

§ See *Mystical Philisophy and Spirit Manifestions*. Being selections from the Correspondences between Saint-Martin and Baron de Liebistorf, 1863.

who have had access to other memorials, and by no means challenge his own, have thrown a curious light on some of his views and findings.\* But there seems no question as to the end of the story.

The Rite of Elect Priests had not only its Sovereign Tribunal at Paris, its active centres at Bordeaux and Lyons, but Lodges in various places were in some way attached thereto, when Martines de Pasqually was called to the West Indies on personal business and left France—*pour aller recueillir une succession*—on May 5, 1772. He died at Port-au-Prince on September 20, 1774. In this manner the medium of communication, Magus or whatever he may be called, was removed from the Rite. The Rituals thereunto belonging and some remarkable catechisms attached to the Grades remained, but the phenomena within the secret circles passed into suspension. The most active members of the Order seem to have regarded it as in a state of paralysis, and even thought that its extinction was at hand. The body-general of Elect Priests at Lyons went over to the Rite of the Strict Observance, Willermoz, perhaps the most active among the disciples of Pasqually, becoming Provincial Grand Master of Auvergne.† All this notwithstanding, the Order of Elect Priesthood was not destined to perish till it was swallowed up in the Revolution. Moreover, according to the archives,‡ Willermoz began himself to develop some of his master's powers, and they are said to have reached their culmination in the year 1785. The result was that the Unknown Agent reappeared within the circle. Presumably his instructions continued, but in the early part of the year 1790§ one-half of the dictated record is said to have been destroyed by the Agent himself, 'who desired to prevent it falling into the hands of the emissaries of Robespierre, who were making unheard-of efforts to secure the whole'.

---

\* The most drastic of these termed himself Chevalier de la Rose Croissante, and wrote an introduction of nearly 200 pages to *Les Enseignements* of Franz von Baader, already cited.

† Introduction to *Les Enseignements Secrets*, p. liii.

‡ Papus, *Martines de Pasqually*, p. 113.

§ Papus, *Martinésisme, Willermosisme, Martinisme*, p.15

So ends the story of the Elect Priests, for the Revolution was raging already, and—as I have mentioned—it engulfed the Rite.

Enough has been said to justify the general conclusion that it was something which belonged to itself, having neither precursors nor successors in the great field which is covered by the name of Masonry. And now as regards the phenomena affirmed to have been produced: it is stated that they occured in full light, while the manifestations were sufficiently substantial to handle and destroy documents. We may draw circles and inscribe Divine Names therein, may light ceremonial tapers and burn consecrated incense, may observe certain fasts and wear certain ritual clothing, may clear and sanctify the precincts, may 'accompany and terminate the séances' by 'most ardent prayers', and may submit ourselves utterly to 'the will of heaven'—all of which was done by the adept priesthood;* but séances remain séances. My personal certitude is that whatsoever took place in the secret workings of Pasqually's Rite, as all deponents testify, was in virtue of psychic powers possessed by him or by his pupils, and that these powers were identical with those with which we have been familiar for more than fifty years under the name of mediumship. Moreover, as is also the case in phenomena of the modern denomination, Pasqually could by no means invariably command his gifts, and there was one occasion when his complete failure caused him to be regarded as an imposter in a Lodge at Toulouse, from which he was driven forth in disgrace.†

The Abbé Fournié was another disciple of the Rite, who offers a still more signal instance of continuous or recurring mediumship, and we have the advantage of his personal record in a printed book.‡ I have said elsewhere§ that he was filled at an early age with 'an intense desire for a demonstration of the reality of another life and the truth of the central doctrines of Christianity'. He came to know Pasqually and was brought within his occult circle, though it is possible that he did not

---

\* Papus, *Martinésisme*, etc., pp. 14, 15.

† Introduction to *Les Enseignements Secrets*, p. xvi, *et seq.*

‡ *De que nous avons été, ce que nous sommes et ce que nous viendrons*, 1802.

§ *The Unknown Philosopher*, p. 40.

attain the higher grades, and was therefore a stranger to the experiences of the 'Unknown Agent'. He describes himself as a simple unlettered man: 'I have no knowledge of human sciences, without being for such reason opposed to their culture. I have been a student at no time. The only books which I have read are the Holy Scriptures, the Imitation of our Divine Master Jesus Christ, and the book of prayers "in use among Catholics" under the title of *Petit Paroissien.*' He became more and more consumed with the desire of God, more and more haunted with the dread of annihilation. Two years after the death of Pasqually, he heard his voice in the evening, and turning round saw him with his own eyes. 'With him,' the Abbé adds, 'were my father and mother, both also dead in the body.' The conversation which they held together 'might have passed between men and women under ordinary circumstances'. The manifestations continued. He saw the Christ of Nazareth on the Cross of Calvary, afterwards in the resurrection state of Easter, and finally in the glory of Ascension. He saw Mary, the mother of Jesus, and other persons. As regards the visions generally, he says: 'I have beheld them during entire years; I have gone to and fro in their company; they have been with me in the house and out of it; in the night and the day; alone and in the society of others; together with a being not of human kind, speaking one with another after the manner of men'. The inspiration following on the Christ visions enabled him to write his one book with extraordinary celerity. It should be added that he lived to a great age and died probably in London. The work itself is a pious memorial, rather of the nature of reverie, and after translating many passages for the purposes of this notice, I have concluded that there is nothing sufficiently distinctive to demand quotation. So also there is nothing in the Abbé's experiences to distinguish them from natural vision and mediumistic phenomena. The apparitions of the Divine Master were of the picture kind with which we are familiar as much in these days as in the old annals of Christian seership. As regards the Unknown Agent, that final destruction of documents is sufficient of itself to determine in the negative any question of its identity with Him Whom we call Christ or to make us regard seriously the claim that this was a being 'charged with the work of initiation'. Such an ambassador from beyond would have found other ways of checkmating the devices of Robespierre.

Moreover, the whole scheme was frustrated otherwise and came to nothing in the end. The unknown Agent expounding the mysteries of God, man and the universe reminds me somehow of that other Divine Master and Christ of Nazareth Who guided St Catherine of Siena through long years, speaking the language of the Vatican. These things are veridic as experiences, but the mystery concerning them is just this—that while they may be good, and even admirable, within their own measures, they are not that which they seem or that which they may claim to be.

# 7
# THE TEMPLAR ORDERS IN FREEMASONRY
## An Historical Consideration of their Origin and Development

Of all the additional degrees in English Freemasonry, those that combined the Chivalric tradition with Christianity appealed most to Waite, and of them the Order of the Temple held the greatest significance for him. Early in his masonic career, in May 1902, Waite was installed as a Knight Templar in King Edward VII Preceptory No. 173 at London, and in 1905 he was among the founders of the Sancta Maria Preceptory No. 183, becoming its Preceptor in 1909. He was to support the Sancta Maria Preceptory loyally for the rest of his life, acting as Registrar (Secretary) from 1910 to 1940. He also read occasional papers on the history and symbolism of the Order to the members of his Preceptory, and it is one of these—first read in 1925—that is printed here, from the text that was published in *The Occult Review*, Vol. 45, Nos. 1 and 3, in January and March 1927.

HAVING regard to the fact that Emblematic Freemasonry, as it is known and practised at this day, arose from an Operative Guild and within the bosom of a development from certain London Lodges which prior to the year 1717 had their titles in the past of the Guild and recognised its Old Charges, it would seem outside the reasonable likelihood of things that less than forty years after the foundation of Grand Lodge Knightly Orders should begin to be heard of developing under the ægis of the Craft, their titles in some cases being borrowed from the old institutions of Christian Chivalry. It is this, however, which occurred, and the inventions were so successful that they multiplied on every side, from 1754 to the threshold of the French Revolution, new denominations being devised when the old titles were exhausted. There arose in this manner a great tree of Ritual, and it happens, moreover, that we are in position to affirm the kind of root from which it sprang. Twenty years after the date of the London Grand Lodge, and when that of Scotland may not have been twelve months old, the memorable Scottish Freemason, Andrew Michael Ramsay, delivered an historical address in a French Lodge, in the course of which he explained that the Masonic Brotherhood arose in Palestine during the period of the Crusades, under the protection of Christian Knights, with the object of restoring Christian Churches which had been destroyed by Saracens in the Holy Land. For some reason which does not emerge, the foster-mother of Masonry, according to the mind of the hypothesis, was the Chivalry of St John. Ramsay appears to have left the Masonic arena, and he died in the early part of 1743, but his discourse produced a profound impression on French Freemasonry. He offered no evidence, but France undertook to produce it after its own manner and conformably to the spirit of the time by the creation of Rites and Degrees of Masonic Knighthood, no trace of which is to be found prior to the thesis of Ramsay. Their prototypes of course were extant, the Knights of Malta, Knights of the Holy Sepulchre, Knights of St Lazarus, in the gift of the Papal See, and the Order of Christ in Portugal, in the gift of the Portuguese Crown. There is no need to say that these Religious and Military Orders have nothing in common with the Operative Masonry of the past, and when their titles were borrowed for the institution of Masonic Chivalries, it is curious how little the latter owed to the ceremonial of their precursors, in their manners of making and installing Knights, except in so far as the general prototype of all is found in the Roman Pontifical. There are, of course, reflections and analogies: (1) in the old knightly corporations the candidate was required to produce proofs of noble birth, and the Strict Observance demanded these at the beginning, but owing to obvious difficulties is said to have ended by furnishing patents at need; (2) in the Military Order of Hospitallers of the Holy Sepulchre of Jerusalem, he undertook, as in others, to protect the Church of God, with which may be compared modern Masonic injunctions in the Temple and Holy Sepulchre to maintain and defend the Holy Christian Faith; (3) again at his Knighting he was 'made, created and constituted now and for ever', which is identical, word for word, with the formula of another Masonic Chivalry, and will not be unknown to many.

But the appeal of the new foundations was set in another direction, and was either to show that they derived from Masonry or were Masonry itself at the highest, in the proper understanding thereof. When the story of a secret perpetuation of the old Knights Templar—outside the Order of Christ—arose in France or Germany, but as I tend to conclude in France, it was and remains the most notable case in point of this appeal and claim. It rose up within Masonry, and it came about that the Templar element overshadowed the dreams and pretensions of other Masonic Chivalries, or, more correctly, outshone them all. I am dealing here with matters of fact and not proposing to account for the facts themselves within the limits of a single study. The Chevalier Ramsay never spoke of the Templars; his affirmation was that the hypothetical building confraternity of Palestine united ultimately with the Knights of St John of Jerusalem; that it became established in various countries of Europe as the Crusaders drifted back; and that its chief centre in the thirteenth century was Kilwinning in Scotland. But the French or otherwise German Masonic mind went to work upon this thesis, and in presenting the Craft with the credentials of Knightly connections it substituted the Order of the Temple for the chivalry chosen by Ramsay. The Battle of Lepanto and the Siege of Vienna had invested the annals of the St John Knighthood with a great light of valour; but this was as little and next to nothing in comparison with the talismanic attraction which for some reason attached to the Templar name and was obviously thrice magnified when the proposition arose that the great chivalry had continued to exist in secret from the days of Philippe le Bel even to the second half of the eighteenth century. There were other considerations, however, which loomed largely, and especially in regard to the sudden proscription which befell the Order in 1307. Of the trial which followed there were records available to all, in successive editions of the French works of Dupuy, first published in 1654; in the German *Historical Tractatus* of Petrus Puteamus published at Frankfort in 1665; in Gurtler's Latin *Historia Templariorum* of 1691; and in yet other publications prior to 1750. There is not a little evidence of one impression which was produced by these memorials, the notion, namely, of an unexplored realm of mystery extending behind the charges. It was the day of Voltaire, and it happened that a shallow infidelity was characterized by the kind of licence which fosters intellectual extravagance, by a leaning in directions which are generally termed superstitious—though superstition itself was pilloried—and in particular by attraction towards occult arts and supposed hidden knowledge. Advanced persons were ceasing to believe in the priest but were disposed to believe in the sorceror, and the Templars had been accused of magic, of worshipping a strange idol, the last suggestion—for some obscure reason—being not altogether indifferent to many who had slipped the anchor of their faith in God. Beyond these frivolities and the foolish minds that cherished them, there were other persons who were neither in the school of a rather cheap infidelity nor in that of common superstition, but who looked seriously for light to the East and for its imagined traditional wisdom handed down from past ages. They may have been dreamers also, but they were less or more zealous students after their own manner, within their proper measures, and the Templar Chivalry drew them because they deemed it not unlikely that its condemnation by the paramount orthodoxy connoted a suspicion that the old Knighthood had learned in Palestine more than the West could teach. Out of such elements were begotten some at least of the Templar Rites and they grew from more to more, till this particular aspect culminated in the Templar dramas of Werner, in which an Order concealed through the ages and perpetuated through saintly custodians reveals to a chosen few among Knights Templar some part of its secret doctrine—the identity of Christ and Horus, of Mary the Mother of God, and Isis and the Queen of Heaven. The root of these dreams on doctrine and myth transfigured through the ages—with a heart of reality behind it—will be found, as it seems to me, in occult derivations from Templar Ritual which belong to *circa* 1782 and are still in vigilant custody on the continent of Europe. I mention this lest it should be thought that the intimations of a German poet, though he was an active member of the Strict Observance, were mere inventions of an imaginative mind.

There is no historical evidence for the existence of any Templar perpetuation story prior to the Oration of Ramsay, just as there is no question that all documents produced by the French non-Masonic Order of the Temple, founded in the early years of the nineteenth century, are inventions of that period and are fraudulent like the rest of its claims, its list of Grand Masters included. There is further—as we have observed—no evidence of any Rite or Degree of Masonic Chivalry prior to 1737, to which date is referred the discourse of Ramsay. That this was the original impetus which led to their production may be regarded as beyond dispute, and it was the case especially with Masonic Templar revivals. Their thesis was his thesis varied. For example, according to the Rite of the Strict Observance the proscribed Order was carried by its Marshal, Pierre d'Aumont, who escaped with a few other Knights to the Isles of Scotland, disguised as Operative Masons. They remained there and under the same veil the Templars continued to exist in secret from generation to generation under the shadow of the mythical Mount Heredom of Kilwinning. To whatever date the old dreams ascribe it, when Emblematic Freemasonry emerged it was—*ex hypothesi*—a product of the union between Knights Templar and ancient Scottish Masonry. Such is the story told.

The Strict Observance was founded by Baron von Hund in Germany between about 1751 and 1754 or 1755, and is usually regarded as the first Masonic Chivalry which put forward the story of Templar perpetuation. I have accepted this view on my own part, but subject to his claim at its value—if any—that he had been made a Knight of the Temple in France, some twelve years previously. The question arises, therefore, as to the fact or possibility of antecedent Degrees of the kind in that country, and we are confronted at once by many stories afloat concerning the Chapter of Clermont, the foundation of which at Paris is referred to several dates. It was in existence, according to Yarker, at some undetermined period before 1742, for at that date its Masonic Rite, consisting of three Degrees superposed on those of the Craft, was taken to Hamburg. A certain Von Marshall, whose name belongs to the history of the Strict Observance, had been admitted in the previous year, Von Hund himself following in 1743—not at Hamburg, but at Paris—for all of which no authority is cited and imagination may seem to have been at work. But some of the statements, including those of other English writers are referable to a source in Thory's *Acta Latamorum*. When Woodford speaks of Von Hund's admission into Templar Masonry at Clermont as not a matter of hypothesis, but of certain knowledge, he is dependent on the French historian, according to whom the German Baron was made a Mason at Paris in 1742. The Chapter of Clermont was founded in that city so late as 1754, and some time subsequently Von Hund returned thither, with the result that he derived Templar teaching from Clermont, on which he built up the Observance system. But, whatever the point is worth, this story is not only at issue with that of Von Hund himself, but with the current chronology of the Observance. To involve matters further, the Chapter is reported otherwise to have derived its Templar element from something unspecified at Lyons which is referred to 1738. The utmost variety of statement will be found, moreover, as to the content of the Clermont Rite, the Templar character of which has been also challenged. It is proposed otherwise that the Chapter was founded on a scale of considerable magnitude, that it was installed in a vast building, and that it attracted the higher classes of French Freemasons, which nothwithstanding it ceased to exist in 1758, being absorbed by the Council of Emperors established in that year for the promulgation of a different Grade system.

I am in a position to reflect some light for the relief of these complications by reference to Dutch archives which have come to my knowledge. The date of the Chapter's foundation remains uncertain, but it was in activity between 1756 and 1763, so that it was not taken over—as Gould suggests—by those Masonic Emperors to whom we are indebted for the first form of the Scottish Rite, Ancient and Accepted. It is not impossible that its foundation is referable to the first of these dates, when it superposed on the three Craft Grades as follows: (1) Grade of Scottish Master of St Andrew of the Thistle, being the fourth Grade of Masonry, 'in which allegory dissolves'; (2) Grade of Sublime Knight of God and of his Temple, being the Fifth and Last Grade of Free Masonry. At a later period, however, it became the Seventh Grade of the Rite, owing to the introduction of an Elect Degree which took the number 5 under the title of Knight of the Eagle, followed by an Illustrious Degree, occupying the sixth place and denominated Knight of the Holy Sepulchre. The Grade final in both enumerations—otherwise Knight of God—presented a peculiar, as it was also an early version of the perpetuation story, from which it follows that the Clermont Rite was Templar.

I have so far failed to trace any copy of the Ritual in this country with the exception of that which has been placed recently in my hands, an example of the discoveries that await research in continental archives. The Templar element—which may be called the historical part—is combined with a part of symbolism, for though allegory is said to be abandoned in the Fourth Degree, its spiritual sister is always present in Ritual. The aspect which it assumed in the present case is otherwise known in Masonry, the Chapter representing the Holy City, the New Jerusalem, with its twelve gates, as a tabernacle of God with men. The Candidate is represented therefore as seeking the light of glory and a perfect recompense, while that which he is promised is an end of toils and trials. He is obligated as at the gates of the City and is promised the Grand Secret of those who abide therein. The City is—spiritually speaking—in the world to come, and the reward of chivalry is there; but there is a reward also on earth within the bonds of the Order, because this is said to be divine and possessed of the treasures of wisdom. The kind of wisdom and the nature of the Great Secret is revealed in the Perpetuation Story, and so far as I am aware offers the only instance of such a claim being made on behalf of the Templars, in or out of Masonry. It belongs to a subject which engrossed the zeal of thousands throughout the seventeenth century and had many disciples—indeed, they were thousands also—during the Masonic Age which followed. The story is that the Templars began in poverty, but Baldwin II, King of Jerusalem, gave them a house in the vicinity of the site where Solomon's Temple was built of old. When it was put in repair by Hugh de Payens and the rest of the first Brethren, their digging operations unearthed an iron casket which contained priceless treasures, and chief among all the true process of the Great Work in Alchemy, the secret of transmuting metals, as communicated to Solomon by the Master Hiram Abiff. So and so only was it possible to account for the wealth of adornment which characterized the First Temple. The discovery explains also the wealth acquired by the Templars, but it led in the end to their destruction. Traitors who knew of the secret, though they had not themselves attained it, revealed the fact to Clement V and Philip the Fair of France, and the real purpose of the persecution which followed was to wrest the transmuting process from the hands of its custodians. Jacques de Molay and his co-heirs died to preserve it, but three of the initiated Knights made their escape and after long wandering from country to country they found refuge in the caves of Mount Heredom. They were succoured by Knights of St Andrew of the Thistle, with whom they made an alliance and on whom they conferred their knowledge. To conceal it from others and yet transmit it through the ages they created the Masonic Order in 1340; but the alchemical secret, which is the physical term of the Mystery, has been ever reserved to those who can emerge from the veils of allegory—that is to say, for the chiefs of St Andrew of the Thistle, who are Princes of the Rosy Cross, and the Grand Council of the Chapter.

The alchemical side of this story is in a similar position to that of the perpetuation myth, of which it is an early version. There is nothing that can be taken seriously. But this is not to say that in either case there is no vestige of possibilities behind. Modern science tends more and more to show us that the transmutation of metals is not an idle dream and—speaking on my own part—there are well-known testimonies in the past on the literal point of fact which I and others have found it difficult to set utterly aside. So also there are few things more certain in history than the survival of Knights Templar after their proscription and suspension as an Order. With this fact in front of us it is not a hypothesis improbable that there or here the chivalry may have been continued in secret by the making of new Knights. It is purely a question of evidence, and this is unhappily wanting. The traditional histories of Knightly Masonic Degrees—like those of the Chapter of Clermont, the Strict Observance and the Swedish Rite—bear all the marks of manufacture; the most that can be said concerning them—and then in the most tentative manner—is that by bare possibility there may have been somewhere in the world a rumour of secret survival, in which case the root matter of their stories would not have been pure invention. The antecedent material would then have been worked over and adapted to Masonic purposes, inspired by the Oration of Ramsay.

It is to be presumed that when this speculation is left to stand at its value, there is no critical mind which will dream of an authentic element in Hugh de Payen's supposed discovery of the Powder of Projection at or about the site of the Jewish Temple. This romantic episode stands last in a series of similar fictions which are to be found in the history of Alchemy. When we are led to infer therefore by the records before me that the Chapter of Clermont reached its end *circa* 1763, we shall infer that it was in a position no longer to carry on the pretence of possessing and being able to communicate at will the Great Secret of Alchemy. It is evident from the Ritual that this was not disclosed to those who, being called in their turn, were admitted to the highest rank and became Knights of God. It was certainly promised, however, at a due season as a reward of merit. From a false pretence of this kind the only way of escape would be found by falling back upon renounced and abjured allegory. Now, we have seen that the Chapter in its last Degree represented the New Jerusalem, and therefore its alchemy might well be transferred from a common work in metals to the spiritual side of Hermeticism. Those who have read Robert Fludd and Jacob Böhme will be acquainted with this aspect; but it may not have satisfied the figurative Knights of God, who had come so far in their journey from the Lodge of Entered Apprentice to a Temple of supposed adeptship. The Chapter therefore died.

I have met with another French Ritual in a great manuscript collection and again—so far as ascertained—it seems to be the sole copy in England, though it is not unknown by name, in view of the bibliographies of Kloss and Wolfsteig. It is called *Le Chevalier du Temple*, and is of high importance to our subject. The collection to which I refer is in twelve volumes, written on old rag paper, the watermark of which shows royal arms and the lilies of France: it is pre-French Revolution and post 1768—say, on a venture, about 1772. The Ritual to which I refer extends from p. 73 to 202 of the fifth volume, in a size corresponding to what is termed crown octavo among us. The hand is clear and educated. The particular Templar Chivalry is represented as an Order connected with and acknowledging nothing else in Freemasonry except the Craft Degrees. In respect of antiquity it claims descent by succession from certain Canons or Knights of the Holy Sepulchre, who first bore the Red Cross on their hearts, and were founded by James the First, brother of the first Bishop of Jerusalem. These Canons became the Knights Hospitallers of a much later date. On these followed the Templars, from whom the Masonic Knights of the Temple more especially claimed derivation, though in some obscure manner they held descent from all, possibly in virtue of spiritual consanguinity postulated between the various Christian chivalries of Palestine. The traditional history of the Grade is given at unusual length and is firstly that of the Templars, from their foundation to their sudden fall, the accusations against them included; it is a moderately accurate summary, all things considered. There is presented in the second place a peculiar version of the perpetuation story which is designed on the one hand to indicate the fact of survival in several directions, and on the other to make it clear that Templar Masonry had in view no scheme of vengeance against Popes and Kings. After the proscription of the chivalry it is affirmed that those who remained over were scattered through various countries, desolate and rejected everywhere. A few in their desperation joined together for reprisals, but their conspiracy is characterized as detestable and its memory is held in horror. It fell to pieces speedily for want of recruits. Among the other unfortunate Knights who had escaped destruction, a certain number entered also into a secret alliance and chose as time went on their suitable successors among persons of noble and gentle birth, with a view to perpetuate the Order and in the hope at some favourable epoch that they would be restored to their former glory and re-enter into their possessions. We hear nothing of Kilwinning or Heredom, and indeed no one country is designated as a place of asylum; but it is affirmed that this group of survivors created Freemasonry and its three Craft Degrees to conceal from their enemies the fact that the Chivalry was still in being and to test aspirants who entered the ranks, so that none but those who were found to be of true worth and fidelity should be advanced from the Third Degree into that which lay beyond. To such as were successful the existence of the secret chivalry became known only at the end of seven years, three of which were passed as Apprentice, two as Companion or Fellow Craft, and two as Master Mason. It was on the same conditions and with the same objects that the Order in the eighteenth century was prepared to receive Masons who had been proved into that which was denominated the Illustrious Grade and Order of Knights of the Temple of Jerusalem.

The Candidate undertakes in his Obligation to do all in his power for the glorious restoration of the Order; to succour his Brethren in their need; to visit the poor, the sick and the imprisoned; to love his King and his religion; to maintain the State; to be ever ready in his heart for all sacrifice in the cause of the faith of Christ, for the good of His Church and its faithful.

The Pledge is taken on the knees, facing a tomb of black marble which represents that of Molay, the last Grand Master and martyr-in-chief of the Order. Thereafter the inward meaning of the three Craft Degrees is explained to the Candidate. That of Apprentice recalls the earliest of Christian chivalries, being the Canons or Knights of the Holy Sepulchre, who for long had no distinctive clothing and hence the divested state of the Masonic Postulant. But this state signified also that his arm is ever ready to do battle with the enemies of the Holy Christian Religion and his heart for the sacrifice of his entire being to Jesus Christ. The alleged correspondences and meanings are developed at some length, but it will be sufficient to mention that the Masonic Candidate entered the Lodge poor and penniless, because that was the condition at their beginning of the Templars and the other Orders of Christian Knighthood.

The Candidate is prepared for the Second Craft Degree in a somewhat different manner from that of the First, and this has reference to certain distinctions between the clothing of a Knight of the Holy Sepulchre and that of a knight of St John. The seven steps are emblematic of the seven sacraments of the Holy Church, by the help of which the Christian Chivalries maintained their faith against the infidel, and also of the seven deadly sins which they trampled under their feet. The Blazing Star inscribed with the letter *Yod*, being the initial letter of the name of God in Hebrew, signified the Divine Light which enlightened the Chivalries and was ever before their eyes, as it must be also present for ever before the mind's eye of the Masonic Templars, a sacred symbol placed in the centre of the building. In French Freemasonry the Pillar B belonged to the Second Degree and was marked with this letter, which had reference to Baldwin, King of Jerusalem, who provided a House for the Templars in the Holy City.

The Traditional History of the Master Grade is that of the martyrdom of Jacques de Molay, the last Grand Master of the Temple. The three assassins answered to Philip the Fair, Pope Clement V and the Prior of Montfaucon, a Templar of Toulouse, who is represented as undergoing a sentence of imprisonment for life at Paris on account of his crimes, by the authority of the Grand Master. He is said to have betrayed the Order by making false accusations and thus secured his release. The initials of certain Master Words are J.B.M., and they are those also of Jacobus Burgundus Molay.

The *Chevalier du Temple* has unfortunately no history, so far as I have been able to trace. I have met with it as a bare title in one other early collection, which has become known to me by means of a Dutch list of MSS, and there is no need to say that it occurs in the nomenclature of Ragon. It is numbered 69 in the archives of the Metropolitan Chapter of France, and 8 in the Rite of the Philalethes: they may or may not refer to the same Ritual as that which I have summarized here. There is no means of knowing. In any case the 36th Grade of Mizraim and the 34th of Memphis, which became No. 13 in the Ancient and Primitive Rite, is to be distinguished utterly: it is called Knight of the Temple, but has no concern with the Templars and is quite worthless. It should be added that in one of the discourses belonging to *Le Chevalier du Temple* there is a hostile allusion to the existing multiplicity of Masonic and psuedo-Masonic Grades, and this may suggest that it is late in the order of time. A great many were, however, in evidence by and before the year 1759. We should remember Gould's opinion that there was an early and extensive propagation of *Ecossais* Grades, and the source of these was obviously in the Ramsay hypothesis. It is certain also that *Elu* Grades were not far in the rear. The date of the particular *Collection Maçonnique* on which I depend is, of course, not that of its contents. On the whole there seems nothing to militate against a tentative or provisional hypothesis that *Chevalier du Temple* was no later and may have been a little earlier than the Clermont Knight of God, this giving further colour to the idea that Templar Masonry and its perpetuation story arose where it might have been expected that they would arise, in France and not in Germany. I have said that the Grade under notice has no reference to Scotland or to any specific place of Templar refuge after the proscription. But the chivalrous origin of Masonry is not less a Ramsay myth, and it characterizes almost every variant of Templar perpetuation which has arisen under a Masonic ægis, from that of the Knights of God and the *Chevalier du Temple* to that of Werner and his *Sons of the Valley*, belonging to the year 1803. There stand apart only the English Religious and Military Order and the late French Order of the Temple which depends from the Charter of Larmenius, but this was not Masonic, though its pretence of Templar perpetuation and succession is most obviously borrowed from Masonry. In conclusion, I shall think always that Baron von Hund drew from France, whether directly at Paris or via Hamburg in his own country.

We have seen that the Strict Observance appeared in Germany between 1751 and 1755, a development according to its founder of something which he had received in France so far back as 1743. No reliance can be placed on this statement, nor is the year 1751 in a much better position. Hund is supposed to have founded a Chapter of his Templar Rite about that time on his own estate at Unwurdi, where the scheme of the Order was worked out. We hear also of a later scheme, belonging to 1755 and dealing with financial matters. But the first evidential document is a *Plan of the Strict Observance*, laying claim on January 13, 1766, as its date of formulation and there is a record of the Observance Master Grade, with a Catechism attached thereto, belonging to the same year. But as 1751 seems too early for anything in the definite sense so 1766 is much too late. A memoir of Herr von Kleefeld by J. C. Schubert bears witness to the former's activities on behalf of the Strict Observance between 1763 and 1768. The Rite, moreover, was sufficiently important in 1763 for an imposter named Johnson to advance his claims upon it and to summon a Congress at Altenberg in May, 1764, as an authorized ambassador of the Secret Headship or Sovereign Chapter in Scotland. His mission was to organize the Order in Germany, and for a time Von Hund accepted and submitted, from which it follows that his own Rite was still in very early stages. I make no doubt that it made a beginning privately *circa* 1755, and that a few persons were knighted, but Von Hund had enough on his hands owing to the seven years' war, so that from 1756 to 1763 there could have been little opportunity for Templar Grades under his custody, either on his own estates or elsewhere. Meanwhile the Clermont Rite was spreading in Germany and in 1763 there were fifteen Chapters in all. There is hence an element which seems nearer certitude rather than mere speculation in proposing that the Templar claim on Masonry was imported from France into Germany, that Von Hund's business was to derive and vary, not to create the thesis. Of the great success which awaited the Strict Observance, once it was fairly launched, of its bid for supremacy over all continental Masonry and of the doom which befell it because no investigation could substantiate any of its claims, there is no opportunity to speak here. It may be said that a final judgment was pronounced against it in 1782 when the Congress of Wilhelmsbad set aside the Templar claim and approved the Rectified Rite, otherwise a transformed Strict Observance, created within the bosom of the Loge de Bienfaisance at Lyons and ratified at a Congress held in that city prior to the assembly at Wilhelmsbad. The Grades of the Strict Observance superposed on the Craft were those of Scottish Master, Novice and Knight Templar; those of the revision comprised a *Régime Ecossais*, described as Ancient and Rectified, and an *Ordre Intérieur* being, Novice and Knight Beneficent of the Holy City. It laid claim on a spiritual consanguinity only in respect of the Templar Chivalry, apart from succession and historical connection, but it retained a certain root, the poetic development of which is in Werner's *Sons of the Valley* already mentioned, being the existence from time immemorial of a Secret Order of Wise Masters in Palestine devoted to the work of initiation for the building of a spiritual city and as such the power behind the Temple, as it was also behind Masonry.

In conclusion as to this part of my subject, the combined influence of the Templar element in the Chapter of Clermont and that of the Strict Observance which superseded it had an influence on all Continental Masonry which was not only wide and general, but lasting in the sense that some part of it has persisted there and here to the present day. The eighth Degree of the Swedish Rite, being that of Master of the Temple, communicated its particular version of the perpetuation myth, being (1) that Molay revealed to his nephew Beaujeu, shortly before his death, the Rituals and Treasures of the Order; (2) that the latter escaped, apparently, with these and with the disinterred ashes of the master, and was accompanied by nine other Knights, all disguised as Masons; (3) that they found refuge among the stonemasons. It is said that in Denmark the history of Masonry, owing to the activity of a Mason named Schubert, became practically that of the Observance, until 1785, when the Rectified Rite was introduced as an outcome of the Congress of Wilhelmsbad. It was not until 1853 that the Swedish Rite replaced all others, by reason of a royal decree. So late as 1817 the Rectified Rite erected a central body in Brussels. In 1765 the Observance entered Russia and was followed by the Swedish Rite on an authorized basis in 1775.

Poland and Lithuania became a diocese of the Observance Order in 1770, and it took over the Warsaw Lodges in 1773. The story of its influence in Germany itself is beyond my scope. It is written at large everywhere: at Hamburg from 1765, when Schubert founded an independent Prefectory, to 1781 (when the Rectified Rite was established for a brief period by Prince Karl von Hesse); at Nuremberg in 1765, under the same auspices; in the Grand Lodge of Saxony from *circa* 1762 to 1782; at Berlin, in the Mother Lodge of the Three Globes, from 1766 to 1779, when the Rosicrucians intervened; at Konisberg from 1769 to 1799 in the Provincial Grand Lodge; in the Kingdom of Hanover, at the English Provincial Grand Lodge, from 1766 to 1778; and even now the list is not exhausted. The explanation of this influence through all its period and everywhere is (1) that which lay behind the romantic thesis of Ramsay, as shown by his work on the *Philosophical Principles of Natural and Revealed Religion*, published in 1748—I refer to the notion that there was a Mystery of Hidden Knowledge perpetuated in the East from the days of Noah and the Flood; (2) that which lay behind, as already mentioned, the talismanic attraction exercised on Masonic minds in the eighteenth century by the names of Knights Templar, because the Church had accused them. They had learned strange things in the East: for some it corresponded to the view of Ramsay, for others to occult knowledge on the side of Magic, and for the Chapter of Clermont to Alchemy. The collapse of the Strict Observance was not so much because it could not produce its hypothetical unknown superiors, but because it could not exhibit one shred or vestige of the desired secret knowledge.

I have now accounted at length for that which antecedes the present English Military and Religious Order of the Temple and Holy Sepulchre, so far as possible within the limits at my disposal. The Clerical Knights Templar, which originated at Weimar with the Lutheran theologian, J. A. von Starck, and presented its claims on superior and exclusive knowledge to the consideration of the Strict Observance about 1770, represent an intervention of that period which has been judged—justly or not—without any knowledge of the vast mass of material which belongs thereto and of which I in particular had not even dreamed. The fact at least of its existence is now before me, and I await an opportunity to examine it. I can say only at the moment that it was devised, as my reference shows, to create an impression that an alleged Spiritual Branch of the old Knights Templar possessed their real secrets and had been perpetuated to modern times. It was, therefore, in a position to supply what the Strict Observance itself wanted; but the alleged Mysteries of the Order appear to be those of Paracelsus and of Kabalism on the magical side. I have left over also: (1) *Les Chevaliers de la Palestine*, otherwise Knights of Jerusalem, because although it is a Templar Grade, it is concerned with the old chivalry at an early period of its history, and not with its transmission to modern times; (2) the Grade of Grand Inspector, otherwise Kadosh, though I am acquainted with a very early and unknown Ritual, because it does not add to our knowledge in respect of the Templar claim on Masonry. In the earliest form it shows that the judgement incurred by those who betrayed, spoliated and destroyed the Order had been imposed Divinely; that the hour of vengeance was therefore fulfilled, and that the call of Kadosh Knights was to extirpate within them those evil tendencies which would betray, spoliate and destroy the soul. (3) Sublime Prince of the Royal Secret, because in the sources with which I am acquainted it recites the migrations of Templars and only concerns us in so far as it reproduces and varies the Ramsay thesis in respect of Masonic connections. It is important from this point of view. (4) Sovereign Grand Inspector General, because I have failed so far to meet with any early codex, and that of Ragon is a Templar Grade indeed but concerned more especially with wreaking a ridiculous vengeance on the Knights of Malta, to whom some of the Templar possessions were assigned. (5) Knight Commander of the Templar, because, according to the plenary Ritual in manuscript of Albert Pike, it is exceedingly late and is concerned in his version with the foundation and history of the Teutonic Chivalry, which is beside our purpose.

In respect of the English Military and Religious Order I have met with nothing which gives the least colour to a supposition of Gould that it arose in France: the *Chevalier du Temple* is its nearest analogy in that country, but the likeness resides in the fact that both Orders or Degrees have a certain memorial in the centre of the Chapter or Preceptory: we know that which it represents in at least one case and in the other, as we have seen, it is the tomb of the last Grand Master. But failing an origin in

France it is still less likely that it originated elsewhere on the continent, as, for example, in Germany. I conclude, therefore, that it is of British birth and growth, though so far as records are concerned it is first mentioned in America, in the Minutes of a Royal Arch Chapter, dated August 28, 1769. I have sought to go further back and so far have failed. It was certainly working at Bristol in 1772, and two years later is heard of in Ireland. It is a matter of deep regret that I can contribute nothing to so interesting and vital a question, which appeals expecially to myself on account of the beauty and spiritual significance of the Ritual in all its varied forms. The number of these may be a source of surprise to many, and I have pointed out elsewhere that however widely and strangely they differ from each other they have two points of agreement: there is no traditional history presenting a perpetuation myth or a claim on the past of chivalry, while except in one very late instance, there is no historical account whatever; and they are concerned with the one original Templar purpose, that of guarding the Holy Sepulchre and pilgrims to the Holy Places. They offer no version of Masonic origins, no explanation of Craft Symbolism, no suggestion of a secret science behind the Temple, no plan of restoring the Order to its former glory, and, above all, to its former possessions. The issue is direct and simple, much too simple and far too direct for a Continental source. Moreover, the kind of issue would have found no appeal in France, for example, or Germany, because there was no longer any need in fact to guard the tomb of Christ, and there were no pilgrims in the sense of crusading times. Finally, they would not have allegorized on subjects of this kind.

I am acquainted personally with nine codices of the Ritual, outside those which belong to Irish workings, past and present, an opportunity to examine which I am hoping to find. The most important are briefly these: (1) That of the Baldwyn Encampment at Bristol, which is probably the oldest of all: the procedure takes place while a vast army of Saracens is massing outside the Encampment. (2) That of the Early Grand Rite of Scotland, subsequently merged in the Scottish Chapter General: the Pilgrim comes to lay the sins and follies of a lifetime at the foot of the Cross, and he passes through various symbolical veils by which the encampment is guarded. (3) That connected with the name of Canongate Kilwinning under the title of Knight

Templar Masonry, in which there is a pilgrimage to Jericho and the Jordan. (4) That of St George Aboyne Templar Encampment at Aberdeen, a strange elaborate pageant, in which the Candidate has a searching examination on matters of Christian doctrine. (5) That of the Royal, Exalted, Military and Holy Order of Knights of the Temple, in the library of Grand Lodge. It represents a revision of working and belongs to the year 1830. It is of importance as a stage in the development of the English Military Order. (6) That which Matthew Cooke presented to Albert Pike, by whom it was printed in the year 1851. It is practically the same as ours and was ratified at Grand Conclave on April 11 of that year. (7) That of the Religious and Military Order, of the grace and beauty of which I have no need to speak. The two that remain over are Dominion Rituals of the Order of the Temple, being that in use by the Sovereign Great Prior of Canada prior to 1876, and that which was adopted at this date under the auspices of the Grand Master, Wm. J. B. MacLeod Moore. They are of considerable interest as variants of the English original, but the second differs from all other codices by the introduction of three historical discourses, dealing with the origin of the Templar Chivalry, its destruction and its alleged Masonic connections, which subject to critical examination, the conclusion reached being that the Templar system is Masonic only in the sense that none but Masons are admitted. The appeal of the entire sequence is one and the same throughout, an allegory of human life considered as pilgrimage and warfare, with a reward at the end in Christ for those who have walked after His commandments under the standard of Christian Chivalry.

We have very little need to make a choice between them, either on the score of antiquity or that of Ritual appeal. A descent from the Knights Templar is of course implied throughout, but it is possible to accept this, not indeed according to the literal and historical sense, but in that of the relation of symbols. The old Chivalry was founded and existed to defend the Church and its Hallows, and Masonic Knights Templar are dedicated to the same ends though official obediences alter and Hallows transform. The Holy Sepulchre for them is the Church of Christ, however understood, and if there is anything in the old notion that the Christian Chivalry in the past had sounded strange wells of doctrine, far in the holy East, there are such wells awaiting our own exploration, to the extent that we can enter into the life behind doctrine, and this is the life which is in Christ. Finally the modern chivalry is of Masons as well as Templars, because in both Orders there is a quest to follow and attain. But this Quest is one, a Quest for the Word, which is Christ, and a Quest for the Abodes of the Blessed, where the Word and the Soul are one.

# 8
# THE GRADE OF KADOSH

The Grade of Knight Kadosh is the 30th Degree of the Ancient and Accepted Scottish Rite, but despite his membership of the Rite Waite took a curious dislike to the Grade—especially as presented by Albert Pike, the Sovereign Grand Commander of the Rite in its Southern Jurisdiction of the USA. The account of the Rite given in the *New Encyclopaedia of Freemasonry* is both hostile and inaccurate, but the text printed here is that of the previously unpublished version of the entry, duly revised and corrected, that Waite prepared for the intended 'new edition' of the *Encyclopaedia*. It is still a hostile account and it is ironic that late in his life, in November 1935, Waite received the 30th degree himself.

FROM whatever point of view we may approach it, this Grade is of considerable consequence and has a curious history in Masonry. It has suffered as many transformations as that of ROSE-CROIX, though not for the same reason. The story that it was invented at Lyons in 1743 appears to be without foundation, and there are several other myths as to the date and circumstances of its origin. In the present state of our knowledge they must be left open questions. Had the COUNCIL OF EMPERORS OF THE EAST AND WEST come into existence in 1758 with its full complement of twenty-five Degrees, the KADOSH would have been extant at that date, but we do not know its exact dimensions at the beginning nor the periods of its successive possible extensions. As regards the Grade under notice, I have described in my *Emblematic Freemasonry*, pp. 199 *et seq.*, a manuscript Ritual which is either the original itself or immediate next thereto, and have shown that it is a Templar Grade, in which the Order of the Temple is spiritualized, while the work of the Candidate is to extirpate evil from his own nature and not to wreak vengeance on others. With this light behind us we may proceed to consider further texts.

**Motive and Purpose**. The earliest KADOSH account which I have traced is that of Le Franc in LE VOILE LEVÉ POUR LES CURIEUX, but there is a slightly anterior record of Monjoie which I know at second hand only. He records that in the course of its ceremonial the Duc d'Orléans had to cast himself bodily from a ladder. However this may be, it is certain (1) that the best known and most developed codices subjected the Candidate to severe trials as a test of his endurance, and (2) that they were concerned on the surface at least with avenging the death of Molay, Grand Master of the Temple, on the temporal and spiritual powers represented by Philippe le Bel and Pope Clement. In this manner there arises the question of Grade-motive, and it seems exceedingly plausible to affirm that those who devised it aimed at the destruction of monarchical government in France and of the Catholic Religion. Under the auspices of Gérard Encausse, all French Martinism adopted this view at the end of the nineteenth century. Put quite simply, the thesis was that the Templar Grades en masse aimed at revolution in France and that the French Revolution came. On the whole, it is much too plausible to be quite convincing, and the hypothesis over-reached itself by seeking to include too much. There is nothing more certain in Masonic history than is the freedom of the Templar STRICT OBSERVANCE from any political taint, while in respect of religion it is sufficient to say that Baron von Hund, its creator to all intents and purposes, was reconciled to the Latin Church, for reasons connected with the Rite, when it was almost at the zenith of European power and influence. At a later period the French ORDRE DU TEMPLE, depending from the Charter of Larmenius, had some leaning for a period towards jobbery in heretical religion, which caused a fissure in the Rite, but it had no cause in politics. The MILITARY AND RELIGIOUS ORDER, which arose in England, so far as it is possible to say, and was certainly unheard of on the Continent during the eighteenth century, was from the beginning and remains now a high Catholic Grade without one tincture of concern in questions of earthly royalty. In the eighteenth century the Templar Grade of KADOSH may be said to stand alone, with little to account for its inclusion in the sequence of the COUNCIL

OF EMPERORS, wherein it is heard of first. The SUBLIME PRINCE OF THE ROYAL SECRET is its supplement and figures later on in the same series. It is known only by comparatively late recensions, through the modifications and added pretensions of which there appears to emerge the original design of the Grade, being the old alleged Templar dream of rebuilding the Temple in Jerusalem: there is no vengeance motive, no cause against King or Pope. And lastly when the time came to devise or transform the Grade final of the SCOTTISH RITE, being that of SOVEREIGN GRAND INSPECTOR GENERAL, the alleged object was to wreak vengeance, as we shall see, on the KNIGHTS OF MALTA, to whom the treasures of the Temple had passed and from whom they must be wrested. It is the aftermath of the KADOSH judgment on the 'sanguinary criminals' who proscribed the Order and martyred its illustrious members. After this manner did the job in revolution pass out by descent into the simple ridiculous, and a day of small things followed, when the Grade of KADOSH was philosophized, talking many platitudes under the ægis of MEMPHIS and MIZRAIM. On account of its historical importance in the scheme of High Grade Masonry, let us observe how it stands ritually at three periods, according to successive deponents.

**Views and Judgments.** The KADOSH is the regenerated man, for whom all ambiguity ceases, according to Abbé Barruel, whose account—though confessedly at second hand—does not differ essentially from antecedent reports of Lefrance and Cadet Gassicourt, on the hostile side, or indeed those of Thory and Reghellini, save only in respect of the design, with which I am concerned no further. We hear of a darksome cave, wherein the Candidate was left to himself, with ropes about him; of subterranean passages, of ascent performed in the darkness; of a sudden fall—though it involved no real danger; or a ceremonial vengeance achieved; of a solemn obligation taken with a pistol at the breast; and—after these ordeals—the ends and purpose of the Grade revealed. It is of course at this point that Barruel introduces his own personal views—the reduction of kings and pontiffs to the common level of citizens. There is not the least reason to suppose that the Ritual—whatever its concealed purpose—betrayed itself in this maner. There is not the least reason to admit Thory's statement that the Degree was invented at Lyons in 1743: Kloss and the German HANDBOOK alike lean towards its rejection. Its position one hundred years later is shewn clearly by Clavel when he says (1) that it cursed the memory of Philippe le Bel, Clement V and the traitor Noffodei; (2) that they were termed the three abominables; (3) that the Candidate ascended a ladder of seven steps; but so far from being steps of vengeance and revolution (4) that they were inscribed with the words Charity, Candour, Mildness, Truth, Perfection, Patience and Discretion. It is therefore obvious that although the Grade in France had suffered some considerable revision as time went on, we are not confronted by elements which suggest that anarchy was stewing in a Masonic cookshop. If we elect to believe that the Knights Templar were nursing mothers to Emblematic Freemasonry or devised and assumed at their suppression the figurative veils of the later Order, it is not surprising and not especially significant that the wicked king and the venal pope should be cursed in two or three versions of a Masonic Grade. It may not be a wise proceeding after the lapse of centuries; but High or any other Grades of Masonry are not wells of wisdom. It remains to say that the so-called KADOSH of Martinism, KADOSH of the Jesuits, KADOSH of the first Christians and KADOSH of the STRICT OBSERVANCE are figments of imagination. About 1860 Ragon produced a Philosophical Grade which he described as designed to replace the Templar Degree of the SCOTTISH RITE, on the ground that this was passing out of use. The proposed purpose was to make men virtuous and happy. The vengeance motive disappeared, and the Sanctuary became one of peace. The Candidate was called upon to express his views on civilization, the world beyond, pre-existence, good and evil, etc. He ascended a ladder, the steps of which represented the seven planets, the order being—Saturn, Venus, Jupiter, Mercury, Mars, Moon, Sun; but what the progression signified and why the planets were appropriate symbols within the conception of the Grade I do not pretend to know. It was held to represent Rectified and Rationalized Masonry, but it was in every respect negligible.

**Pike's Reconstruction.** In the recension of Albert Pike the three abominables have become two wretches, being the particular Pope and King, while the vengeance of the past has become a punishment of crime. I do not propose to describe the secret workings, as we are concerned with their representative principles and not with dramatic procedure; but it may be certified that certain pirated versions printed in America are utterly at fault respecting the main episodes. No knight lies mystically dead and within a coffin, but being dead yet speaketh: no skulls are stabbed by the Candidate. It is said in the authentic codex that 'the death of De Molay and the destruction of his Order call for no other vengeance at our hands than that we should, if possible, prevent the recurrence of such deeds'. It is a Grade of great expiation in which the Candidate is pledged to punish crime and protect innocence. He is taken from apartment to apartment, oath is piled upon oath, while ever and continually he is threatened with the dreadful ordeals involved by his determination to proceed. By the hypothesis, he persists however, while from room to room and from pledge to pledge the 'great instruction' that is said to replace symbols grows from more to more in the perfection of all banality, the historical illustration being designed only to enforce the necessity of union in order to resist tyranny and unmask imposture. It does not follow in the logic of the endless verbiage that Kings are symbols of tyranny or Popes of imposition. Nothing indeed follows, because nothing is specified; though the word appears to be groaning under a dual 'disgraceful yoke'. In one word, the Pike recension is the Grade of KADOSH reduced to the *ne plus ultra* of foolish pretence. The Grand Elect Knights of the eighteenth century would have known where they were, if ever they had undertaken explicitly or otherwise to destroy royalty and religion, but when they play now at destructions in the names of liberty, equality and fraternity, no one knows where he is, or in what sense he is saluted as Sacred or Holy Knight, Knight of the White and Black Eagle, and Grand Elect Knight. Better the PHILOSOPHIC KADOSH of the Grand Orient—when it happened to have a KADOSH—better MEMPHIS and MIZRAIM, 'false in sentiment and fictitious in story', than the deep below the deep in this gulf of unreason.

# 9
# THE SPIRITUAL SYMBOLISM OF FREEMASONRY
## An Introduction to C.B.C.S.

Early in 1903 Waite travelled to Geneva to receive the Grades of Novice and *Chevalier Bienfaisant de la Cité Sainte* (Knight Beneficent of the Holy City) in the *Rite Écossais Rectifié* (Scottish Rectified Rite), the Rite that he saw as 'the head and Crown of Masonry'. He later received the degrees of *Profès* and *Grand Profès*, but it was the grade of Knight of the Holy City that contained for him the very essence of the Secret Tradition in Freemasonry. It was, he said, a 'great and holy Grade of Christian Knighthood spiritualized', and it inspired him to write the following *Introduction* to his translation of *The Liturgy of the Rite of the Strict Observance*. Although both translation and introduction had been prepared in 1905, they were not printed until 1934, when a small number of copies was issued in the USA. The *Introduction* was reprinted in 1946 in *Nocalore* (the *Transactions* of the North Carolina Lodge of Research), under the heading *An Introduction to C.B.C.S.*— But this is an equally misleading title as far as the general reader is concerned, for the essay contains rather the essence of Waite's understanding of masonry as a whole. To avoid further confusion I have given the essay a new and, I trust, more appropriate title.

THROUGH all the centuries the great fathers and teachers of the Church mystic have sounded in the ears of their disciples the doctrine of the insufficiency of outward things, but at the same time they have recognized, nor has any school of thought more strongly insisted on, the symbolical importance of all that by which we are encompassed externally. The Church mystic is made up of numerous confraternities to each of which there is assigned, or by each has been created, a certain characteristic tissue of symbolism by means of which their peculiar instruction has received an outward shape and vesture. In this manner we have the symbolism of doctrine, which is delivered always, because it can be delivered only, by way of economy or approximation; we have also the symbolism of the literary forms assured by mystic thought, and in the schools of Christian mysticism, some of these have been elaborated to an extraordinary degree; we have the symbolism of rite and ceremony; and there are other veils and emblazonments which will occur to the reader. The truth is that ideas in the absolute order are conceived only by representation, which is the mode of symbols and sacraments. There is in the soul of man an undoubted desire to over-reach this ministry of representation and to obtain an immediate experience and it is in this sense that he and his true interpreters the mystics are anxious of the insufficiency of the several external orders—as for example the Church and the world by which he is initiated and passed till the time comes for his raising from the symbolical death of this material life out of the lesser mysteries into the great mysteries of the Third Degree. But the great teachers who are immortal are not for that reason infallible and their lessons of insufficiency have more often than not been drawn from a sense of the drunkenness and aberration which the outward things produce in humanity at large because humanity has for want of any proper criterion accepted their ministry indiscriminately. The awakening of the sense of symbolism is the awakening from this state of intoxication and the first gift which it bestows upon the things without is the sense of a great significance behind which indeed there is almost an infinite diversity, an unmeasured depth and wealth which to the poet is the source of inspiration, to the seer the spring of prophecy, to the mystic the great font of correspondences by which he forges the great chains of union binding all worlds together. There is therefore no ground for the insufficiency of external objects as regards the ministry of their symbolism, but the chaotic ministry to undiscerning and simple sense is of course insufficient and as already said there is a grade in which the mind can no longer be satisfied by its representations. Whether there is any field for their satisfaction of the desire which is thus awakened, perhaps no mystic can tell us, but it accounts for the extreme sadness, apart from all passions of the mind which in fine settles down upon thought in the highest places, striving after that Infinite which eludes us. In either case there can be no doubt that the chief concern of mysticism is to satisfy the hunger and thirst after righteousness which is awakened under the proper ministry of symbolism, the term righteousness being taken in its true sense as the direction of the whole man towards the absolute goodness, thus differing widely from the common acceptations which connect it with standards of morality less or more conventional, the prescripts of social decency, or conformity with the ceremonial requirements of the several systems of religious belief. These things are also sacramental and until their service has been accepted indiscriminately they can signify very little to the life of the soul.

Our considerations so far are those which are universal in application, but if we descend to things particular we must be prepared to find that some instituted systems of symbolism, however discriminate are insufficient, some signs have ceased to signify, some modes of representation are vain and trivial. We cannot, for example attach importance, as aids towards rightousness, to mysteries founded on mythologies the dispensations of which have passed away or to systems of ceremonial designed to inculcate things which are already generally admitted, are obvious or elementary in their nature or which can be taught better by a direct method. The institutes of ordinary morality, for instance, are an improper subject for symbolism, and a sacramental institution, a dramatic mystery, a mode of ceremonial initiation which exists simply to inculcate such institutes or to lay special stress on charity, fraternity, equality, freedom, relief and even the abstract notion of truth by recourse to the veils of allegory and the illustrations of symbolism mobilizes too great a force to accomplish too slight a purpose as from our earliest childhood we have been taught these virtues more simply, more directly and hence better by the catechisms of all the churches, nor does it appear that the more cumbrous method more surely conduces to the end. To teach duties which are transparent to everyone by the help of very complex machinery does not do outrage to the good sense of many and perhaps the majority of persons as the general mind of the world is only just emerging from the ethical period both in literature and art and the story with a moral, the picture which reads a homily, the poem which furnishes a good example is no less ridiculous than the three or the three and thirty grades of a system which boasts as its solid foundation the practice of the moral and social virtues. We are not belittling these virtues or denying the need to practice them, but we affirm that having been passed, raised, exalted, installed and enthroned there is a sense of disparity in learning that the last secrets are like the first secrets, those of universal benevolence.

It is not therefore surprising that many thoughtful persons who are members of the various associations which inculcate morality in symbolism, or in other words the obvious by the not obvious, should confess secretly or otherwise to a consciousness of insufficiency. When describing this insufficiency recourse has been had to the Masonic terminology, though Masonry is not the only association to which the remark applies. It has, however, a peculiar position in comparison with all others, for its symbols, its perfect ceremonies and its craft legends indicate almost unmistakeably that they were designed originally to convey other subjects of instruction. The sacramental edifice seems to be like the 'columns left apart of a Temple once complete'. It is an excellent and incontrovertible truth that an angle of ninety degrees is the fourth part of a circle, but a story illustrating this elementary fact of geometry belongs to the region of trivia; the admitted code of ethics is also excellent and incontestable, but it does not lend itself to symbolism and if we find in the Masonic symbolism much which is unexplainable by elementary geometry or by the common maxims of morality we have the right to look further and every student of the fraternity will be justified at once by the haunting sense that throughout its modern rituals there are certain elements which are not modern, there are certain affiliations and allusions which take us back through all the Christian centuries, even to Eleusis and to Egypt. The mystery surrounding these elements constitutes in these days the only real secret of Masonry, except indeed the rise and origin of the symbolical craft itself but this is another aspect of the same mystery. It is therefore true to say that the Masonic secret is not taught in lodges or in any manner communicated to initiates but is discovered, if it is ever discovered, by the initiate for himself and that this being so the adepts in Masonry are exceedingly few, that is, those who are admitted to the Adepta, though the postulants at the threshold are innumerable.

From this point of view let us glance as briefly as possible both at the symbols and the central legend. In the first place let us observe the train of thought occasioned by the two pillars Jakin and Bohas which are at the entrance, so to speak, of the Masonic

Temple. From the account in the First Book of Kings it might seem to follow that the erection of these pillars was an afterthought on the part of King Solomon and though this is scarcely borne out by the collateral account in Chronicles, while their description in the first place is exceedingly elaborate, it can scarcely be said that there is anything in Holy Scripture which would cause us to single out these objects as particular representatives of an art of building spiritualized, even if that art was grouped about the central figures of the first Temple of the Jews. In seeking therefore to understand how this importance came to be attributed to the two pillars we are justified in asking whether any other system of symbolized teaching, prior to the appearance of speculative Masonry on the horizon of history, laid special stress on the mystical importance of the two Pillars and an answer is ready to our hand in Kabalism. Here let us pause for a moment over a few words of preliminary consideration. We know that the three degrees of Craft Masonry, together with the Royal Arch, in the form that we at present possess them deal only with the Jewish side of the Divine dispensations and that they contain references and legendary matter which if they are not the inventions of modern times are also not to be found in the writings of the Old Testament. We know also that the writings called Kabalistic constitute with the Talmud the great storehouses of Jewish tradition and Jewish wisdom. It is not therefore idle to expect that some light may be cast on the Masonic symbols and legends by reference to these sources. This being granted, I will place in the hands of the reader a translation of two texts which will in all probability be unknown to him, as they will also at first be unintelligible:

'Jakin is the name of the right pillar which Solomon made in the sanctuary and it corresponds to the measure of NETZACH. But NETZACH rejoices in this name because MALKUTH is established by JACHIN. To this all the commentators agree and it would seem for the following reason, namely, that by JACHIN the efflux of CHESED is sent down by MALKUTH whereby the bride is adorned that she may be lovely and desirable in the eyes of the bridegroom. It may be asked, however, why it is not termed MAKIN, the present tense rather than JAKIN the future. The reason is that beyond this present firmament there is another which shall be established, as if to say that however He establishes the one the other shall continually lend strength.

Such is the mind of the commentators. But to me the Redemption seems signified, the beginning whereof shall be from NETZACH. For Rabbi Simeon ben Jochai says that the beginning of Redemption is from the Aurora, whence shall follow the morning. Here by Aurora is understood NETZACH. And because Solomon knew that the Temple should be destroyed, he set up this column, which he called JACHIN, as if to say: He shall erect and prepare the House and He shall help redemption. See the *Garden of Pomegranates*, Tract XXIII, c.10. And in the *Gates of Light* it is said as follows concerning this name: Solomon made the right column, which he called JACHIN, in reference to NETZACH, to which the name JEDUD TSABOTH is referred. And he who knows the mysteries of the two columns, which are JACHIN and BOAZ, shall understand after what manner the NESHAMOTH or minds descend with the RUACHOTH or the spirits and the NEPHASOTH or the Souls by EL-CHAI and ADONAI through the influx of these two columns. Hence the description in I Kings VIII, 15, of the two columns; of the two capitals, v 16; and of the entablatures. The columns are NETZACH and HOD, the capitals GEDULAH and GEBURAH and the entablatures are CHOKMAH and BINAH. By these two columns and by EL-CHAI the minds and Spirits and Souls descend, as by their passages or channels. And by the column JACHIN shall be built and erected the city of Zion, which is Jerusalem, as it is said in Ps. LX, 11, where if the words—Thou shalt clothe the poor in thy goodness—be really understood, it will be known also after what manner NETZACH prepares and sends down benefits in EL-CHAI, that it may pour every influence and benediction into MALKUTH, which is void, even as the poor man who possesses nothing. This is also the meaning of Gen. I, 9. Know also that from this place is the disposition of all the forms and configurations of all things formless, that so all ATZILUTH may be joined with ADONAI. So also, in fine, does every member of man receive the form of its disposition from this place. Whence it is said in Deut. XXXII, 6—Hath he not made thee and formed thee?

So far as regards the right pillar, and in respect of the left we are told:

BOAZ is HOD, for it was in respect of this SEPHIRA that the left column was placed in the Temple of Solomon. The sense is to be sought in Ps. LXVIII, 35—He that giveth strength and power—from this foundation, because the influx is exercised from GEBURAH ... In the *Gates of Light* this name is thus connected with HOD: In reference to the measure of Hod, Solomon made the second column, which he called BOAZ, and hereto pertain the mystic words of the Canticle v, 15: His legs are as pillars of marble, set upon sockets of fine gold. The legs are NETZACH and HOD, whereunto are attributed the Names ZEDUD TSABAOTH and ELOHIM TSABAOTH. For these grades are the columns of the SEPHIROTH and beholding these, Solomon caused the two columns of JACHIN and BOAZ to be made. But as regards the pillars of marble mentioned in the Canticle it should be noted that the central line is the mystery of the mode of TIPHERETH, to which the letter VAU in the great Name of God is attributed. Hence these two columns are placed under the said letter of the TETRAGRAM which is mystically denoted by the Hebrew equivalent of flax, in allusion to the Hexad and bears six Names, which are GEDULAH, GEBURAH, TIPHERETH, NETZACH, HOD and JESOD. Therefore NETZACH and HOD are the pillars of the letter VAU, and they are placed over JESOD as JESOD over the foundation or Throne, the Name of which is ADNI. For, according to the text of the Canticle, the pillars of marble are based upon sockets of fine gold, symbolically signifying the mode of JESOD and referring to the Name ADONAI. The seven lower SEPHIROTH are therefore bound up in this text *his legs are as pillars of marble,* being GEDULAH, GEBURAH, TIPHERETH, NETZACH and HOD; SET is JESOD, the foundation, while *sockets of gold* is the seventh measure which is called ADNI. But from the place of these six SEPHIROTH were created those two Seraphim mentioned in Isaiah, VI, 2, who are called Lords of six wings. They are also termed Seraphim, that is, burning or consuming because they consume all who are not zealous for the glory of God while they study the work of the Chariot and are occupied over the mystery of CHASMAI. They also consume those who practice arts by the name of the Crown. These are also the fonts and sources whence flow the six clauses of the Mishnah, till it reaches the measure of Adonai, which is called the oral law. And because these two columns are those of the HEXAD, to them is referred the mystery of the two tables, connecting the written law, contained in these tables with the oral law comprised in six classes. And whosoever advances in the study of the written and oral law conjoins the Tabernacle so that it is made one and unites the Blessed Name and the mystery of JACHIN and BOAZ. Lastly, BOAZ receives its strength from GEBURAH and its vigour from Binah, and therefrom do flow all kinds of Power and of emanation and of rigour appertaining to Judgment and Fear; and by virtue of the said measure doth Adonai abide in the Glory of the Kingdom'.

These quotations the remarkable nature of which will not be immediately recognized by the conversed reader are not derived at first hand from the Hebrew Kabalists, but from a Latin elucidation in which the originals are considerably simplified. The jargon is still barbarous and the sense so obscure that it will be scarcely believed to exist, yet an explanation sufficient for our purpose can be given in a few words. The Kabalistic system of philosophy supposes four worlds, those of pure Deity, of Formation, Creation and of things material and infra-material. Each of these worlds is produced from the extension of ten modes emanated successively, termed SEPHIROTH, and grouped after the following manner:

THE CROWN

| INTELLIGENCE | | WISDOM |
|---|---|---|
| SEVERITY | | MERCY |
| | BEAUTY | |
| VICTORY | | GLORY |
| | FOUNDATION | |
| | KINGDOM | |

Three columns or pillars are thus formed, that on the right hand being symbolized by Jachin, which was the right in the porch of the Temple and that on the left by Boaz, the left-hand pillar of Solomon. The Divine, Intellectual and Animal principles which constitute the complete man descend or are evoked through Jachin to be manifested in the Kingdom, which is this present external world. This world will in the end pass away or be transformed, a change symbolized under the notion of a new firmament and also the heavenly or spiritual Zion. We see therefore that the Kabalists were builders in imagination of a city not made with hands and hence in their own degree they observe the mystic title of speculative Masons.

The left hand pillar, or Boaz, is more especially referred to the written and oral law, the union of which is the Key to the mystery of Jachin and Boaz, and thus the Kabalists in addition to an occult purpose cherished a secret knowledge concealed by the sense of a written and literal knowledge, that is to say, a system veiled in allegory and illustrated by symbols. We do not err therefore in supposing that Masonry is enlightened by Kabalism, seeing that in this respect they have a common symbolism, an analogous purpose and the kinship of a similar claim. If, as I believe, the art and craft of Masonry was once concerned with other mysteries than those of an elementary good conduct, if through paths difficult of exploration it did attempt to follow nature and science, if, in particular, there were practical reasons from the nature of the Masonic experiment why it should require of its candidates a belief in God and in a resurrection to a future life, then assuredly this connection of Jakin and Boaz with the history of the human soul, its origin, transmigration and destiny, and with the secret doctrine concerned paramountly therewith, does offer to those who can tolerate such investigations, a view of the Masonic purpose *ab origine symboli* which removes the sense of insufficiency awakened by its imputed purpose. I do not suggest that Masonry is to be identified with Kabalism; crudities of this kind are offences of a bygone day; but having regard to the sources from which the Jewish Theosophy was derived, it is not impossible that it transmitted something to Masonry and that those who gave to symbolical architecture its mysterious passwords had personal knowledge that a wisdom was treasured in Jewry outside the Law and the Prophets.

But if such are the results of an exceedingly slight inquiry into the symbolism of the two pillars at the entrance of the Temple of Solomon, more may be reasonably expected from a consideration of the Temple itself, that eternal memory of Israel. I suppose that a day will come when we shall cease to regard its legend as a building made with hands or in abandoning the literal record to look upon it as less inspired because its truth is in a higher sense. If, adhering closely and intelligently to the account given in Esdras, we should come to see that what was destroyed at the epoch of the Captivity was a secret doctrine of Israel, we shall approach the mind of Israel as exhibited in the vast literature of the Christian centuries.

The world for the Kabalists was full of palaces and each of these was the Temple of Solomon idealized and returned into the archetypal world. The universe itself was at once palace and temple and the visible creation in particular, this lower world, the sphere of *Malkuth* or the kingdom was viewed as the Temple of *Adonai* and the abode of the Cohabiting Glory, or *Shekinah*, and the Temple of the material Zion in which the Presence was manifested, also under the name of Shekinah, was thus the image of the world. It will be seen how readily this conception lent itself to the institution of multitudinous analogies in the fervid mind of Jewry, how this microcosmic marvel of the builder's art signified now the body of man enlightened by the indwelling spirit, which was also the understanding of the Law, and now the spiritual Jerusalem; how in its destruction it was the secret doctrine laid waste by the advocates of the letter, or again the chosen nation, the peculiar people, delivered into the hands of idolaters; and finally, if we may for a moment plunge more deeply into the complexities of their mysterious system, how the Temple was also for the Kabalists the symbol of the primal world before the serpent had ascended into the Tree of Life; how its destruction typifies the Fall; how the second Temple stands for the restored world of Kabalism which differs from the first in glory and from which the *Shekinah* had receded; how in fine there is a Third Temple which is to come, over which there shall be a new firmament. It is this Temple which the Kabalist, like the Mason, always rebuilt in his heart; and as I know that this splendid spectrum, like the bow of promise, rests over all the late literature of the Temple and over the dreams of all the palaces, I must be permitted to register an inward conviction that here also something has been indirectly derived into Masonry from these spiritual builders of the greater exile. The notion of this influence or transmission creates no rivals because there is nothing exclusive in consideration. I know that long after the golden age of Kabalism, yet far earlier than the earliest date we can assign to the craft rituals, the Rosicrucian Fraternity dreamed of a spiritual temple, while at the very period when the wonder and the rumour of the *Zohar*, or chief work of Kabalism, first astonished the synagogues and ghettos of Spain, there arose that Order of Templars which legend has always accredited with the intention of another Temple. From these sources also something may have been inherited or acquired by speculative Freemasonry, as we shall have ground later on for admitting, but such views do not interfere with one another for there are links of connection and bonds of consanguinity between all these occult systems, and the mystical edifice of the Freemasons is a fabric of many materials originating in strange places of thought, not excepting some of the Christian mystics who spiritualized Solomon's Temple after their own manner from the days of St Augustine and the City of God to those of St Teresa. The office and mission of the Church itself may indeed be similarly regarded, for it is a great temple still in the course of erection which in virtue of its inherent vitality builds itself up from within and is improved and beautified forever by the continual transmutation of its living stones. At the Gate of Initiation the two pillars of the Temple have been from all time a part of the symbolism of the Mysteries, and the Temple, the Holy Place, the Sanctuary within the Sanctuary has signified the mystery itself and the illumination which it imparts to the neophyte. By the use of these sacraments the particular initiation of Masonry is in communion with universal initiation and is a daughter of the secret knowledge of the past. If the craft rituals have come to us from the operative guilds these guilds connect in some inexplicable manner with the cultus of Isis and Osiris, with the Book of the Dead, with Rabbinical Theosophy and with the legends of Christian Rosenkreutz. But we shall understand this connection better if we have the courage to assume that some crude mystery of the working builders was assumed and transfigured by later makers of ritual who know why the Pillars J and B are at the entrance of every true Temple of initiation and that the House of Solomon spiritualized was never made with hands.

By the next point in our investigation we are led to the passwords of the several degrees, of which it is possible to speak only in vague and general terms. We know that in the third degree the words of the Master Mason are recognized as lost and that others are therefore substituted 'till time or circumstances shall restore the genuine'. In the ceremony of the Royal

Arch this restoration takes place ostensibly but the arcanum communicated therein is that which is recognized by the occult philosophy of the past as in itself a substitution and on this point the Master Mason may be referred to all the literature of the Kabalistic tradition on the subject of the divine Tetrad, the great and holy name which by the grandeur of its power governs all worlds. Peace has departed from the sanctuary and Light out of the Holy Place; the Holy Building remains unfinished; and the divine Temple can be erected only in the heart because this name is lost and is read therefore as Elohim, also 'till time or circumstances' shall restore the true Word and manifest the mystery of the union between Justice and Mercy.

In regard to those symbols of Masonry which for the sake of convenience may here be called pictorial, the most obvious and the least significant are derived from the operative art and though it is possible by an exercise of subtlety to read into these much more than they contain naturally they may be left to inculcate those conventional lessons which the rituals themselves attribute to them. There are others, such as Jacob's Ladder, which belongs to a higher order of symbolism and by this in particular we are again referred to the Kabalists, for whom the *scalam stantem super terram et cacumen illius tengens coelum*, signifies not only the just man whose feet are on earth while his head is in heaven but is in the line of transcension by which Malkuth, or the Kingdom of this world, is taken up into Tiphereth or the Kingdom which is not of this world, being the place of the King in his beauty. But these analogies might be multiplied still further and the most striking have been among several the pentalpha and the six-pointed star, the seal of the microcosm and the seal referred to Solomon. The employment of these symbols is universal in occult science and the explanation of the significance occupies an important part in its literature. They are indeed the most widely diffused of all the magical symbols. As regards the former it is interesting to note that it is the only ancient emblem which Dr Thomas Inman, after many researches, found himself unable to interpret. In the present place there can of course be no attempt to give an account of its history through the ages or to deal adequately with its sacramental value. In Indian symbolism, it is said to represent the conjunction of Brahma and Seeva, and thus, even in the far East it was a sign of equilibrium which is a palmary meaning appointed to it by occult writers in the West. A Pythagorean origin has sometimes been ascribed to it, and it may have been derived by Pythagoras from oriental sources, but the historical evidence is wanting to countenance its connection with his name. It has been described as the badge of the Jewish nation and it connects among the Kabalists with Tiphereth which also connects the microcosm. It has been found engraved upon Jewish tombs in the Roman catacombs. It was one of the Templar emblems and has been thought to be identical with the mysterious symbol prescribed in the *Diagramma* of the Ophites for presentation by the ascending soul to the Genius of each succeeding sphere so as to obtain an unimpeded passage to the supernal light. Lastly, this same symbol has been discovered among prehistoric remains in the New World. The pentagram has externally five acute and internally five obtuse angles and therefore consists of an outer and an inner pentangle. To the inner pentangle great mysteries are ascribed by Cornelius Agrippa. The period of its introduction into Masonry is a matter of dispute; by some it is regarded as an early and by others as a late emblem. There is no need to say that it is familiar to the student of Masons' Marks. While, for the fraternity it is a symbol of health or physical equilibrium, for occult science it represents Man in his entirety and the domination of the spirit, signified by the three upper points. Reversed for the purpose of Black Magic it represents the contrary of these ideas, namely, the demon and the materialization of spirit.

The symbol of the Hexagram, unlike that of the Pentalpha is almost exclusively Jewish, though it may not have originated in Israel, and it is frequently met with in Kabalistic parchment talismans and manuscripts of the middle ages. It has of course been naturalized on most Christian soils and has been derived from Jewry into Islam. Though known usually as the seal of Solomon, it has also been termed the shield of David, which for the Kabalists signifies the covenant by a graceful though unsubstantial analogy. Finally, it is not entirely unknown to India; it is found on some Gnostic gems and, like the five-pointed star is met with occasionally in old books of alchemy, though both emblems can scarcely be regarded as characteristic of the Hermetic department of occult literature. It signifies for occult sciences the circulation of life from heaven to earth and from earth to heaven and therefore illustrates the correspondence between things above and below.

It has been impossible to dispense with these details, though the enumeration is wearisome and does not lend itself to a decorative sense in literature. I must add, out of justice to my standpoint, that these emblems which we have agreed to call pictorial are of no account to the mystic whose symbols belong to different modes of representation. Such signs in the last resources are like the barbarous words made use of in magic; they communicate nothing and are idols rather than sacraments. I have dwelt upon them in detail to shew that stars from strange heavens of thought have risen upon the horizon of Masonry.

It is possible that in the last resource the columns J and B with all the significance attached to them by the higher sense of Jewry are not of the first importance and though deep down in the heart of every Mason there is a consciousness which tells him that the Words of Life have been lost, it is possible also that the legend of the building word which perished with Hiram Abiff, despite its strong appeal, might be insufficient to redeem Masonry as a system from the sense of insufficiency; but the aspiration after the house not made with hands lifts it into the field of mystical activity which is covered by the greater mysteries. We know thereby for what reason the Lodge symbolizes the temple of the material universe and why every candidate for initiation must believe in a resurrection to a future life. It is because the Son of the Widow is called out of the Egypt of this world, through the everlasting portals, into a world of light. This raising in the transcendental order is exhibited by the raising of the Third Degree and is communicated by its great and supreme legend. It is here that the illuminated student is compelled to part company with those for whom speculative Masonry is the daughter of the operative craft, for he knows that all the great initiations raise their candidates out of a symbolic death into the company of those who have been dead with him and are now alive for ever more. The secret history of this initiation has been written once and for all time in the gospels, but the legend of the Third Degree is also that of the Book of the Dead, of the Greek Mysteries, of the sacred myths of India and even of Christian Rosenkreutz. It is rendered after another manner, with great beauty and significance, in the rites of certain secret societies which now exist in the West.

We have now reached a defined stage in these particular

pleadings. In common with those who deserve to be called our brethren we have confessed to a sense of insufficiency in respect to the ostensible purposes and interests of the Masonic experiment, but we have seen that another purpose and a higher concern underlie these and we find that the second sense of craft mystery does not in reality differ from those great mysteries of the past which claimed to communicate to their adepts that which from all time has been understood by the word illumination, by which the individual soul enjoys a certain measure of the universal life. Let us therefore have the courage of our convictions and define speculative Masonry as a hieroglyphical abstract or itinerary of the reintegration of mind in God and postulate this definition as our enlightened construction of the statement in the catechism—that it is a beautiful system of morality veiled in allegory and illustrated by symbols. For the one definition does not destroy the other; the conventional answer is true and so true that those who repeat it seldom realize its significance, because they interpret morality only after an elementary and artificial manner as if it were embraced by good conduct, which is the first step only in that science which the mystic Thomas Vaughan once termed 'both ancient and infinite'. I am too well aware that the measure of the fullness of the stature of this doctrine is, even for its preliminary realization in the logical understanding, outside the possibility of many and I speak therefore only to a small assembly of the elect and of those who are capable of election within the ranks of the fraternity, not doubting that the larger concourse which remains in the letter of the symbol, as in the porch of the spiritual temple, are also in the grace of the symbol, and are takers according to their capacity by a certain light and leading which shall befit them in the age-long process of initiation for the greater ends. In the meantime let those who can suffer these sayings recall in their hearts once again the perfect ceremonies of these degrees and review them in the light of this greater construction, from the 'Brethren assist me to open the Lodge', when all rise to participate in the sacramental ceremony, to the consummation of the Third Degree when 'it is closed accordingly' because this mystery is ostensibly finished, and they will begin to comprehend what is meant in the 'Questions before Raising' by the 'hidden mysteries of nature and science', as well as the kind of house which is established in strength to stand firm for ever.

Whether the position of Masonry which we have thus philosophically stated can be historically justified, or can at least, as an irreducible minimum, be made to harmonize with Masonic history, is a grave question which next presses for consideration. For a space which approaches almost two centuries there has been, as we know, a wide feeling that Masonry is part of the universal system of initiation and that this system was an esoteric religion which existed behind the external religion of several countries and periods. We have not therefore been concerned with a novel standpoint though it has been looked at in a new manner. The esoteric history of Freemasonry remains to be written at large and a sketch of its position, having much that is necessarily tentative, can alone be attempted here. Let us take, in the first place, the naked fact that we do not know: (a) How symbolical Masonry arose; (b) How Craft Masonry passed into symbolical; (c) How its rituals grew up. It is certain, on the other hand, that symbolical lodges existed in the seventeenth century; that the Craft Lodges in Scotland became symbolical; and that there were originally but two degrees. Wherever the practical element prevailed it was completely replaced, but in the case of many old lodges, especially in England, no such element can be shown to have existed. We are led irresistibly to infer that the speculative art was transfigured out of the craft, but it is difficult to affirm certainly that it was not an importation from without, the work of men who had never hewn stones or had part in the erection of houses made with hands. Symbolical Masonry may by no intolerable hypothesis have existed for long years side by side with the operative and may have obtained a direct connection therewith only in historical times. There are some respects in which it may be regarded as a thing which was made rather than a thing which grew. It is in any case certain that the rituals bear no trace of the practice though they are full of its moralities.

The following hypotheses concerning the origin of speculative Masonry have been regarded as possible:

a. that it is the last transfiguration of the simple mystery of the old building guilds.

b. that the notions and terms of architecture were assumed in a metaphorical sense by a secret group of philosophical students and that the final elaboration of this device is found in certain rituals of the 18th century.

c. that the medieval building guilds were direct descendants of the architectural fraternities of antiquity whose members were true initiates and that there was therefore always a speculative or mystical element in Masonry.

d. that the Knights Templar to whom the mystical traditions of antiquity had been communicated in the East assumed the disguise of Masonry after their suppression and were the actual inventors of the speculative art.

e. that speculative Masonry was the last transfiguration of the Rosicrucian Fraternity, or that it was the invention of certain members belonging thereto.

The third hypothesis is now rightly set aside as fantastic; the fifth is a variant of particularization of the second; the fourth is that which has enlisted the most interest and obtained the most general credence among all the legendary attributions and it is entitled to peculiar respect as the prevailing belief of the high grades which broadly speaking may be said to have originated in the idea of chivalry. The first, which has the seal of mediocrity and the general air of common sense, is particularly adapted to those minds which are contented to regard Masonry as a ceremonialized system of morality and it is the accepted explanation, in one of its several forms, of the Masonic historian as we find him at the present day. It has obtained wide diffusion in Germany through the work of Findel and in England through the large history of R. F. Gould.

Those who are convinced that Masonry, by its rites and symbolism, is identical in purpose with the universal object of initiation, will look with suspicion on the attempt to refer it in respect of its origin to a trade guild and it was perhaps this sense of unfitness which prompted the French makers of Masonic legend to assume that the old Temple builders were a secret confraternity perpetuated through many centuries, who in Egypt, Assyria, Judea, in Greece and Rome, erected holy houses for the mysteries in which they also participated; and subsequently in the Christian period erected all over Europe the cathedral churches of Christendom, but still maintaining in mystery not only the peculiar secrets of their building art—the words of the master-builder—but also the spiritual and religious mysteries of Thebes and Eleusis, of Isis, Dionysius and Ceres. These are reveries of the romantic spirit with no particle of historical basis, but they illustrate the reluctance of the past to connect great institutes of symbolism with trade unions and they are right in the sentiment which inspired them however mistaken in fact.

Having reached personally the conclusions set out in the preceding pages, I was prepared to accept what seemed to follow irresistibly from these, the inadequacy, namely, of the first hypothesis which I have scheduled above. Now it must be remembered that secret societies have no history in the strict sense of the term; they do not hand down literature, collect archives, or preserve minutes. In those even which are of recent constitution, it is not less than astonishing how the circumstances of their first incorporation and the incidents of their early years pass into doubt and obscurity. At this day certainly the Masonic lodge has its records and can therefore give account of itself at least in a certain manner, though the old lodges as a rule can tell us little of their early history; but the past of the Masonic, in common with other secret confraternities is speculative like the science which it preserves; in other words, its reconstruction is largely hypothetical, and there are many respects in which the received explanation as to the origin of Masonry rests on evidence which is not less slender than the rejected explanations which prevail in the high grades. In other words, if speculative Masonry is the last transfiguration of some old rite belonging to the building guilds, the conditions of such transfiguration are as much outside our knowledge as the circumstances under which Templarism or Rosicrucianism became changed into or assumed the veil of Masonry, supposing that we accept the hypothesis of its Templar or Rosicrucian origin. The received opinion of the present time has not therefore the marks of finality and the whole question stands therefore liable to be reopened by any new facts which may be brought to light by research. In an excursus appended to the proceedings of the fourth convocation of the Rosicrucian chapter of research, the reports of which body are given in the subsequent pages, I have attempted to establish a tentative connection between the Masonic mystery and that which in the Middle Ages was diffused over a considerable part of Europe under the guise of the Grael legend, and I have further connected that legend because it was impossible to do otherwise, with the original Knights Templar. In this manner the Templar hypothesis of Masonry is again reopened, with what result more extended investigations in the future must be left to shew. It offers an example only of several paths of enquiry which still remain to be explored. Another path is the history of the alleged Templar continuation and its connection with Craft Masonry at the beginning of the eighteenth century. By those who regard this continuation as a fiction originating with the Chevalier Ramsay and by those no less who maintain it the circumstances of this period have been most imperfectly considered, and the remark applies almost with equal force to later Templar history, to the criticism of the charter of Larmenius which has never been seen by those who have adjudicated on either side concerning it, to the still later Levitikon and generally to the several branches of the Masonic chivalry in France. A third path of enquiry concerns the history of alchemy as modified by Rosicrucianism during the seventeenth century in England, more especially at the period of Elias Ashmole. The materials for the history of this period are in reality considerable but they have been very imperfectly investigated because they lie chiefly in books and manuscripts which are written in a concealed language, the Key of which is not in the possession of many historical students. Such an inquiry would involve the reconsideration of certain writings of Francis Lord Verulam, the whole works of Dr John Dee and Dr Robert Fludd, as well as the chief German literature of the subject during the seventeenth century.

As the purpose of this introduction is to methodize and resume the findings of the transactions which are hereafter presented, an historical enquiry is outside consideration and is in the present space impossible, but as a conclusion to this speculative excursion into the withdrawn significance of the craft degrees, I shall now endeavour to indicate certain further grounds on which to base a general affirmation that the origin of Masonry must be considered. They are not historical grounds but they are not the less cogent within their particular sphere and as I know that they are paths of research which are still unexplored, I am not without hope in the future that our narrow measure of historical knowledge may be open to increase when time and circumstances furnish the opportunity thereof.

Having sought to shew that Craft Masonry covers a secret experience belonging to the transcendental Order it remains to say that the whole experiment is not comprised in the Craft Degrees or that from the sacramental standpoint they are not in themselves perfect and complete ceremonies as their technical description is sometimes made to affirm. They are as they stand a story without an end and presuppose a further action elsewhere, just as the Greater Mysteries of Antiquity were to be inferred from the Lesser Mysteries and the novice postulated the Knight. This fact is so obvious, it is emblazoned so broadly about the whole horizon of the Third Degree in particular, that one is at a loss to understand the intellectual, much less the philosophical or transcendental position of those who hold that true Masonry is contained in three degrees only. If we make an exception in the case of the French ritualist, Jean Marie Ragon, who had many graces of esoteric knowledge which should have ruled his reason better, this is almost invariably the belief of those brethren who also maintain the operative origin of the speculative art. It is in fact clear that if the craft degrees presuppose other grades which we find subsequently in fragments among the institutes of Masonic chivalry, among purely Christian orders and in secret societies claiming Rosicrucian connections, such a development of an initiatory system could have begun in operative Masonry only on the assumption of a peculiar transmutation having taken place therein; but if we elect to say that the high degrees were invented to complete the craft system we impeach indeed these supplementary rites, but the craft remains a mutilated sacrament, a labour begun in piety but not ended in zeal and we must look elsewhere for its fulfilment.

It must be remembered in the first place, that the Third Degree, although connected with the notion of raising is in fact a degree of death. It is indeed described explicitly as an instruction how to die or as designed to exemplify and enforce that first lesson of Nature and her supreme secret. In consonance therewith we find that the Word of a Master Mason is not merely a word of death, but even one of corruption. The death it is true is that of the faithful servant who may be said to depart in peace, although his departure is violent and untimely, prior to the accomplishment of his work. As regards the raising, which is personal to the candidate only, this is not in reality symbolical of a passage from death to life, or of that which can be mystically understood by the word REUNION which occurs in the ritual, for what is raised is the body of death, and the episode suggests at first sight a certain confusion of symbolism, though this I think is removed by its further consideration in the higher light of mysticism. In any case, while the Mason is traditionally taught to believe in the resurrection of Hiram, the third degree offers no suggestion concerning the raising of the Master Architect. Two things follow, however, in the ceremonial which are of the highest importance. The candidate who has impersonated the Master is informed that the light of Masonry is only a visible darkness, so that the action of drama may in a certain sense be said to move in a dream and the state of inhibition or somnambulism which is a true sacramental description of our material life is that which is exhibited in the raising. Ultimately the new adept retires with the simulacrum only of his desired object, knowing that his great exemplar is dead like Hermes and Orpheus, that his secrets have perished with him, that for this reason the first symbolical Temple was never built with hands and that he possesses only the words of Death in place of the Words of Life.

More than this literal description need not, I think be urged to support the contention that the third degree supposes something afterwards inevitably. As it stands, it is the rite of the Lamp of this Sanctuary placed behind the altar which is native to the mind, but amidst the added difficulties of an explanation which does not explain, a sacrament which does not minister and a light which offers no advantage to the darkness. He is encouraged however to expect the advent of a bright and morning star, bringing peace and consolation, when it may be inferred that the mock secrets will give place to true arcana and the mystae will see their way. We encounter here a survival of the old Christian allusions which had once their place in these mysteries before they fell under the editorship of unitarians and Deists. We pass now to an examination of the Rite and the symbols of the Royal Arch which claim to restore the Lost Word and so as we have already seen, communicate another substitute.

The beauty, sublimity and importance which have been attributed to this degree have suffered considerably in the hands of successive generations of unskilled revisers, by whom the rite has been successfully canonized till, at the present day it is very nearly impossible in its several versions, so far as ceremonial literature is concerned. As regards its mode of working it has been reduced to a servile imitation of the craft degrees, the terminology of which it reproduces at all possible points and it offers in the course of its lectures a peculiar illustration of its antiquity by an apt citation from the 'Universal Prayer' of Pope. Yet these and many other ineptitudes of the bourgeois mind are like the whitewash of the puritan period concealing but not destroying the pictured saints on the walls of our old churches and the design of the ritual can still be discerned beneath them. It illustrates another of the quests which are universal in the mysteries of initiation and the passage of the soul in the course of that search through the shrouded regions of the underworld. As Orpheus in pursuit of Eurydice, the candidate for exaltation goes down to recover the buried sense of the Divine Word and the lost secrets of Masonry spritualized, and, also like Orpheus, he is in each case put off with a shadow, for he returns bearing in his hand the letter which he already possessed. Here is assuredly a profound allegory on which the history of transcendental experience is only a prolonged commentary. It shows that man does not easily escape from the sacraments and that he does not elude his shadow by reversing his position in the sunlight. In a higher order of symbolism it shows also the imminence of the second sense in the letter of the word, or, as Paracelsus says, that he who eats a crust of bread communicates all the elements of the starry heavens. These lessons might be varied almost indefinitely; they will suffice for the present purpose, but there is one of a different kind which follows from the symbolism of the Royal Arch and there is no need to say that, like those already given, it has never entered into the hearts of the makers of Masonic ritual. While the legend of the Third Degree gives account of an event which made the building of the First Temple impossible as it was originally planned, the action of the Arch ceremonial concludes with the preparation of the ground for the second Temple, so that, as far as Masonry is concerned, the true Temple has never been created except in the heart of the Mason. The reason is that the original scheme of human experience became voided by an event which appears under the parable of the fall of man and was replaced by another and lower form of experience. Those who are acquainted with the Kabalistic symbolism will understand me fully if I refer to the three-headed serpent represented by the three murderers of Hiram, and to its ascent in the tree of life as far as DAATH or science, represented by the Master-Builder so that knowledge was cut off from the source of life. Hence all the soul's legends with her sorrows and aspirations and all the sacraments and elementary education of the material world.

Such are the real indications of the Royal Arch Ritual exhibited by mysticism, as *in sanctas ac venerabiles manus* and it cannot be said that I have derogated from any dignity that may remain to it after the process of its modern editing in order to shew that it does not complete the scheme of Masonic initiation. Those who think otherwise, and they include the great majority of the Masonic Brotherhood, have mistaken the part for the whole, the initial stages of spiritual experience for the entire history of the soul and her progress; but they have thus erred in common with numbers of the lesser mystics, for, although the eye is not satified with seeing, the limit of the eye's range is too often its measure of the great world.

The Orpheus of Masonic initiation must bring back other trophies from the quests of the underworld than those which are indicated in the ceremony, whether we interpret them in the high sense which I have indicated above or are content to understand them in the common Masonic acceptation. The Candidate of the Third Degree has suffered a symbolical death and in the Royal Arch he has entered into Limbus, after which he has in some other ceremonial to put on immortality and thus erect for himself 'a house not made with hands, eternal in the heavens', for which he is left here simply preparing the ground. There are of course other ways in which we may understand the sacramental action of the mystery and one of these is indicated hereafter, in the conversations, under the guise of a secret doctrine lost at the symbolical period of the Third Degree and recovered five hundred years subsequently as the historical lecture informs us; but we are brought back notwithstanding to the same point, as the application of the recovered knowledge in no sense can be said to appear.

There are continental grades which, in spite of certain anachronisms, offer an equivalent of the Royal Arch which is more consistent in its symbolism, and a word may be added concerning them in this place. I refer more particularly to the Scottish Master of St Andrew, originally a single degree which was afterwards divided and does indeed fall naturally into two parts. The Candidate for initiation has been occupied since he was raised in the Third Degree, over the plans for the erection of the second Temple, and he comes at length out of the great tribulation of the captivity to rejoin his brethren at Jerusalem and to assist in the great work. He is shewn the ruins of the First Temple and the cause of its destruction is explained to him, with its symbolical application in Masonry. Through his instrumentality the seven-branched candlestick and the Masonic implements are recovered; the altar is again erected; and as in the Royal Arch, he finds the golden lamen inscribed with the Sacred Name, which he pronounces in a loud voice, thus demonstrating its exclusively sacramental nature. The historical discourse completes the reconstruction of the edifice and tells how the sacred fire was restored to the sanctuary.

In the second degree, which is denominated Perfect Master of St Andrew, the resurrection of Hiram is exhibited to the Candidate together with the fulfilment of the whole quest and experiment of Masonry in the vision of the New Jerusalem. At this point the old Law gives place to the new and Jewish symbolism is replaced by that of Christianity. Both these degrees are defective from the dramatic standpoint and leave something to be desired from the sacramental; they have also suffered within recent years from an attempt to edit them in accordance with liberal religion, but while acknowledging these disabilities and confessing that, transcendentally understood, our Royal Arch has occasionally diviner gleams, they offer two advantages—an explicit consciousness of the spiritual applications of the two Temples and a saving realization that no system of initiation based on symbols derived from the first dispensation can be complete unless it conducts the recipient to the higher sacramentalism which succeeded it.

Having established this point, which is the only conclusion possible in the transcendental order, we are led to enquire whether there is anything in English Masonry which can be said to complete that which is left unfinished in the order of the Royal Arch, and for this purpose we must have recourse to the high degrees.

Among those who deny that anything of importance is communicated in these degrees there is a disposition to regard the craft ceremonial as having grown rather than having been devised and all subsequent rites as having been invented designedly to complete what, by their hypothesis, was wanting in the craft. The actual state of knowledge will not permit the historian to make either affirmation. The earliest of the high degrees, as for example the Royal Order of Scotland and Knight Templar, are involved in as much obscurity with respect to the circumstances of their origin, as the precise nature of the extension and elaboration which occurred at the period of Anderson and Desaguliers. Let us therefore rather on our part lay down a general principle which neither dates nor historians can overrule, namely, that in the last resource all ritual is invented and all ritual grows, for in the course of time it is subjected invariably to modification and extension. We have accordingly, and howsoever they have been derived to us, A, the degrees of Craft Masonry, accounting for their existence as a peculiar system of morality veiled in allegory and illustrated by symbols; B, certain high degrees which carry forward the Masonic system of initiation into Christian modes of presentation and have, like the Craft, their particular legend attached to them; C, a crowd of minor rites arising out of both systems and in many cases without a title to existence. Many of the degrees incorporated by the Ancient and Accepted Scottish Rite, and most of the Antient and Primitive come under this head.

The present enquiry may be confined to the Order of Knights Templar, for which the Royal Arch is a necessary qualification; to the Rose Croix, with the supplementary degree of Kadosh; and to the Royal Order of Scotland, which has some claim to be considered as the most ancient of all their systems.

The Order of Masonic Knights Templar makes no reference in its symbols or its ritual to that Lost Word which the Royal Arch is supposed to restore to the Candidate, beyond the condition which is required of him, namely, that he should be in possession of that word, with the sign thereto belonging, in consideration of which and of the trials which he undergoes symbolically, a more perfect development of the word is exhibited to him in a mysterious manner. In this respect therefore the Knightly grade is a natural sequence of the Royal Arch. In common with the other systems of Masonic chivalry, it suffers under the disability arising from its commemoration of the Knights in place of that of the Temple, to which also there is no allusion throughout the degree. It is however presented to the Candidate as a grade of death and resurrection—of death because it guards the sepulchre and of resurrection because

Christ is risen. There is a reference to the Divine Master as the Bright and Morning Star which is no doubt introduced for the definite purpose of making the application intended by the same allusion in a discourse of the Third Degree. The symbolical significance of the ceremonial is not in itself great, and in the ritual it is next to nothing. Something must be allowed for the mystical meaning of the empty sepulchre over which the Knights keep guard but such a meaning may well be more than was intended by the first inventors of the rite; and importance of another order resides in the manner by which the candidate for installation is passed through the preliminary ordeals of pilgrimage, warfare and penance, which he performs by twice three times as the reduction of twice seven and by once as a reduction of three. The deficiencies in the sacramental aspect are shared in common with all the Knightly grades, but from the ceremonial standpoint it is without doubt the most perfect of all; others of greater interest historically are practised abroad, but they will not compare with it in dramatic force. It has also another striking advantage over the rest of the Templar systems; the legend of Jacques de Molay is from the symbolical standpoint the common burden of these, even if we admit its analogies with the martyrdom of the Master-builder; but in English Templary there is no reference to his betrayal, and this because the action of the drama takes places presumably in Crusading times, or between the period of Simon of Syracuse and that of Squin de Florian, the two Iscariots of the Order. At the same time it exemplifies with much consistency the connection of Masonry with Templarism which is the contention of the latter. As in the Grades of St Andrew which have already passed under notice, it is difficult to justify the connection with the patron saint of Scotland, so in Templar grades it is not easy to bridge over the distance in symbolic time between the Second Temple and the Holy Sepulchre and the logical condition of installation in the Knightly Order would be in the eighteenth degree of Rose Croix rather than the Royal Arch. We are precluded, moreover, by its symbolism from regarding it as that mystery of immortality which we are seeking, though it may indicate a step upon the way. It is difficult, however, to affirm with certainty that it communicates anything in the transcendental order.

Both from the dramatic and the symbolical standpoint the

Rose-Croix Grade, or at least that version which is worked under the obedience of the Scottish Rite, is exceedingly faulty in construction and is completely misplaced in the heterogeneous series of degrees which precede and follow it. In time if not in symbolism it should be located after the Royal Arch, which the Scottish Rite is, however, precluded from working. The ceremonial opens at the hour of the Crucifixion and the rending of the veil of the Temple, with the other symbols of destruction signifying the rupture of the sacramental communication between things above and things below. Hiram is replaced by Christ, with whom the Word is lost as it was with the Masonic Master, and the candidate prior to his constitution is deputed to recover it. It is sought by means of the three cardinal virtues, or, in other words, by the ethical virtues of Craft Masonry exalted into religion, and recovery takes place by the several steps of the pilgrimage. The Word thus found does not in the last resource confer anything upon the Candidate, but the ceremonial itself may in a certain sense symbolize the passage through death into an immortal light beyond, and it contains therefore, albeit most imperfectly, some elements of the Rite which we are seeking. The connection with chivalry is of course an anachronism and consists solely in the fact that it confers the Knighthood of the Pelican. There can be no question that under all its disabilities, it marks a step in the development of Masonic symbolism; the Word which was lost with Hiram is found in Christ, or to express it in closer consonance with the spirit of the ceremonial secret doctrine which perished with Christ, also typified by Hiram, is sought amidst confusion and darkness, and yet under angelic guidance, in Hades, whither Christ descended, and is restored, amidst light and gladness, when Christ rises from the grave, in whom also Hiram is given back to the companions of his toil.

So far then as the enquiry has proceeded we have not found in the most widely diffused of the high degrees that perfect ceremonial which completes craft Masonry, but we have found indications and allusions, remanents of secret doctrines, fragments of the greater experiment but not the full process, isolated pillars of the Temple but not the finished spiritual building. So again in the degree of Kadosh, which is the thirtieth of the Scottish Rite and is termed in that system the *ne plus ultra* of Masonry, seemingly for the inscrutable reason that there are three degrees beyond it, there are found some further gleams, as, for example, conception of the Third or spiritual Temple, and the identification of Hiram with Christ in whom the Master Builder is therefore symbolically raised up after death and clothed with immortality. But the suggestion thus indicated is lost in the legend of Jacques de Molay whose incorporation in the cycle of secret mythos of Masonic initiation is brought about at the expense of the mythos. Hence this degree though it opens with a certain solemnity in the hour of secrecy and silence covers a trivial or vain analogy for which with as much excuse we might substitute the martyrdom of King Charles I. I am making these statements not without reluctance and with a full sense of all that they involve and I am speaking also as one who believes that the influence of later Templarism on Freemasonry was far extending and, as already indicated, that the historical aspects of this influence will be demonstrated more completely in the future. But the lines of this demonstration will be to connect more definitely the old order of chivalry with Freemasonry through the common ancestry of both, while the great crime of the thirteenth century, namely, the suppression of the Templars, does not enter into consideration, and though it is natural that it should have been commemorated in those rites which have perpetuated the idea of the Order, or alternately have continued it to modern times, there can be no symbolical importance attributable to such an event. It is a tragedy of history which receives its commemoration in history, but the events shadowed forth in the central mystery of Christendom and in that of the Third Degree lie outside history and are not of space or time. Hence it is a symbolical anachronism to institute a comparison between the literal fact of the immolation of the Grand Master and the death of Hiram or Christ.

There remains only for consideration among the English grades that of the Royal Order of Scotland, which has been regarded by more than one student as the oldest of all and certainly there is evidence to show that it was at work in London at an earlier period than is recorded of any rite outside the craft degrees, with the exception of the Royal Arch. The form of its ritual lends colour to the notion of its antiquity and it is a matter of surprise that it has not received more serious attention at the hands of Masonic critics. There are many difficulties in connection with its historical position and means are wanting for their removal, but even if we accept its tradition its chief claim on our attention is as an early transformation of the Templars, and though exceedingly interesting from this standpoint it does not in its ceremonial or its symbolism advance the Masonic experiment to a higher stage. It remains therefore one of the curiosities of Masonry rather than one of its landmarks.

That which we have failed to find in any measure of completeness among the high grades now at work in England can, however, be sought, not indeed fully and completely but still with much greater success, on the continent of Europe, where at the present day, and possessing also their representatives in England and America under the seal of secrecy, there exist certain rites of Masonry which are the true descendants of the original high grades as conceived and partially developed by the Chevalier Ramsay, who himself may have derived something from Fenelon and the group of mystics who surrounded him.

From the Chevalier Ramsay these rites passed subsequently with various modifications into the Rite of the Strict Observance and were transformed at the convention of Wilhelmsbad, from whence they issued as the Knights Beneficent of the Holy City of Jerusalem. Those who preserve and work them may not understand the whole of their significance, any more than the Grand Lodge of England understands the metaphysical aspects of the two Pillars of the Temple. They may even have tampered with the traditional doctrines which they are pledged to transmit intact, but the scheme of initiation outside the Royal Arch is contained in these almost unknown degrees which not only preserve the true initiation of chivalry but ultimately pass out of Masonry into those more secret assocations whose very names are generally unknown. They exhibit, as in the case of one of them which has already been seen, the resurrection of Hiram; they transfigure the mystery of the Master Builder into the mystery of Christ and although inverted and darkened they show forth the real nature of initiation. The traditional history which they preserve constitutes the harmony of all the Templar legends and they include firstly the logical transition from Royal Arch Masonry to the eighteenth degree of Rose Croix and from the Rose Croix to the Kadosh. It follows from their teaching that the mystery of initiation is complete in Christ; that the first Temple was in the archetypal world and that its plans were voided; and that the third is still in the course of erection. These symbolical

Temples correspond to Adam Kadmon, archetypal and primeval; to the secret doctrine of religion as it was first committed to our fathers, the Israel of God; to the substituted secrets of the written word; and finally to the dispensation of the spirit wherein is pursued the age-long quest for the recovery of the Lost Word. Withdrawn as it may be from the outer sense of these rituals, they in the last analysis direct our minds to that great experience which by many vague hints and uncompleted allusions we know was indicated to the initiates of the old mysteries, an experience granted to man alone in the divine alliance and in the contemplation of the highest unity.

Beyond these exalted grades of Masonry there are others which can only be hinted at and these connect with others whose rites of death and resurrection are not unknown to some persons now living in England. Among these is also celebrated that Rite of Life which alone completes the experiment of Masonry by raising the candidate not only from simulated death which commemorates the Master Architect but from the underworld in which the keys of the lost knowledge are sought in Masonry.

We find therefore as a general conclusion (a) that the sacramental experiences of Craft Masonry are the beginning of an initiation which is complete elsewhere and it is in the light of this fact that we have to reconsider the question of its original connection with the building guilds; (b) that the process of Masonry is developed further in the high grades but is not complete in these; and (c) that the Lost Word of Masonry must be sought in that undemonstrated place wherein its true object is concealed and where also we shall find the secret of its origin.

I believe that those who can enter into the considerations of this thesis will not only agree that they have expelled that sense of insufficiency which was mentioned in the opening but will be forcibly reminded of at least one catholic experience of Masonry, as of a great and abiding presence in some great and holy house of the Lord and man. For myself and the school which I represent it is the sign of the presence which leads man from house to house of initiation, through many symbolical deaths, through many passways of the underworld, that he may at length be truly raised and most truly exalted beyond the sacramental order and may truly know that the speculative Mason is at work upon the erection of a Temple for the same reason that the pontiff is a bridge-builder.

# 10
# SOME DEEPER ASPECTS OF MASONIC SYMBOLISM

This study first appeared in 1915 in the American masonic journal *The Builder*, whose editor, the Revd Joseph Fort Newton, had requested from Waite a series of contributions on symbolism. It was then reprinted as a set lecture in a reading course for Lodges in Iowa, where Waite's name was already familiar from the praise lavished upon his work by Fort Newton in his book *The Builders*—a copy of which was given to every newly made mason under the Grand Lodge of Iowa. As a consequence of the great popularity of *The Builders* (it is still in print today) Waite's reputation as an exponent of the mystical interpretation of Freemasonry has always been higher in America than in Britain.

## PART I

THE subject which I am about to approach is one having certain obvious difficulties, because it is outside the usual horizon of Masonic literature, and requires, therefore, to be put with considerable care, as well as with reasonable prudence. Moreover, it is not easy to do it full justice within the limits of a single lecture. I must ask my Brethren to make allowance beforehand for the fact that I am speaking in good faith, and where the evidence for what I shall affirm does not appear in its fullness, and sometimes scarcely at all, they must believe that I can produce it at need, should the opportunity occur. As a matter of fact, some part of it has appeared in my published writings.

I will introduce the question in hand by a citation which is familiar to us all, as it so happens that it forms a good point of departure:—'But as we are not all operative Masons, but rather Free and Accepted or speculative, we apply these tools to our morals'. With certain variations, these words occur in each of the Craft Degrees, and the analogies are to be found in a few subsidiary Degrees which may be said to arise out of the Craft—as, for example, the Honourable Degree of Mark Master Mason. That which is applied more specially to the working implements of Masonry belongs to our entire building symbolism, whether it is concerned with the erection by the Candidate in his own personality of an edifice or 'superstructure perfect in its parts and honourable to the builder', or, In the Mark Degree, with a house not made with hands, eternal in the heavens, or again with Solomon's Temple spiritualized in the Legend of the Master Degree.

## A System of Morality

It comes about in this manner that Masonry is described elsewhere as 'a peculiar system of morality, veiled in allegory and illustrated by symbols'. I want to tell you, among other things which call for consideration, something about the nature of the building as this is presented to my mind, and about the way in which allegory, symbols and drama all hang together and make for one meaning. It is my design also to show that Craft Masonry incorporates three less or more distinct elements which have been curiously interlinked under the device of symbolical architecture. That interlinking is to some extent artificial, and yet it arises logically, so far as the relation of ideas is concerned.

There is, firstly, the Candidate's own work, wherein he is taught how he should build himself. The method of instruction is practical within its own measures, but as it is so familiar and open, it is not, properly speaking, the subject-matter of a Secret Order. There is, secondly, a building myth, and the manner in which it is put forward involves the Candidate taking part in a dramatic scene, wherein he represents the master-builder of Masonry. There is, thirdly, a Masonic quest, connected with the notion of a Secret Word communicated as an essential part of the Master-Degree in building. This is perhaps the most important and strangest of the three elements; but the quest after the Word is not finished in the Third Degree.

## The First Degree

Let us look for a moment at the Degree of Entered Apprentice, and how things stand with the Candidate when he first comes within the precincts of the Lodge. He comes as one who is 'worthy and well recommended', as if he contained within himself certain elements or materials which are adaptable to a specific purpose. He is described by his conductor as a person who is 'properly prepared'. The fitness implied by the recommendation has reference to something which is within him, but not of necessity obvious or visible on his surface personality. It is not that he is merely a deserving member of society at large. He is this, of course, by the fact that he is admitted; but he is very much more, because Masonry has an object in view respecting his personality—something that can be accomplished in him as a result of his fellowship in the Brotherhood, and by himself. As a matter of truth, it is by both. The 'prepared' state is, however, only external, and all of us know in what precisely it consists.

Now the manner of his preparation for entrance into the Lodge typifies a state which is peculiar to his inward position as a person who has not been initiated. There are other particulars into which I need not enter, but it should be remarked that in respect of his preparation he learns only the meaning of the state of darkness, namely, that he has not yet received the light communicated in Masonry. The significance of those hindrances which place him at a disadvantage, impede his movements, and render him in fact helpless, is much deeper than this. They constitute together an image of coming out from some old condition by being unclothed therefrom—partially at least—and thereafter of entering into a condition that is new and different, in which another kind of light is communicated, and another vesture is to be assumed, and, ultimately, another life entered.

## The Meaning of Initiation

In the first Degree the Candidate's eyes are opened into the representation of a new world, for you must know, of course, that the Lodge itself is a symbol of the world, extending to the four corners, having the height of heaven above and the great depth beneath. The Candidate may think naturally that light has been taken away from him for the purpose of his initiation, has been thereafter restored automatically, when he has gone through a part of the ceremony, and that hence he is only returned to his previous position. Not so. In reality, the light is restored to him in another place; he has put aside old things, has come into things that are new; and he will never pass out of the Lodge as quite the same man that he entered. There is a very true sense in which the particulars of his initiation are in analogy with the process of birth into the physical world. The imputed darkness of his previous existence, amidst the life of the uninitiated world, and the yoke which is placed about him is unquestionably in correspondence with the umbilical cord. You will remember the point at which he is released therefrom—in our English ritual, I mean. I do not wish to press this view, because it belongs of right, in the main, to another region of symbolism, and the procedure in the later Degrees confuses an issue which might be called clear otherwise in the Degree of Entered Apprentice. It is preferable to say that a new light—being that of Masonry—illuminates the world of the Lodge in the midst of which the Candidate is placed; he is penetrated by a fresh experience; and he sees things as they have never been presented to him before. When he retires subsequently for a period, this is like his restoration to light; in the literal sense he resumes that which he set aside, as he is restored to the old light; but in the symbolism it is another environment, a new body of motive, experience, and sphere of duty, attached thereto. He assumes a new vocation in the world.

The question of certain things of a metallic kind, the absence of which plays an important part, is a little difficult from any point of view, though several explanations have been given. The better way toward their understanding is to put aside what is conventional and arbitrary—as, for example, the poverty of spirit and the denuded state of those who have not yet been enriched by the secret knowledge of the Royal and Holy Art. It goes deeper than this and represents the ordinary status of the world, when separated from any higher motive—the world-spirit, the extrinsic titles of recognition, the material standards. The Candidate is now to learn that there is another standard of values, and when he comes again into possession of the old tokens, he is to realize that their most important use is in the cause of others. You know under what striking circumstances this point is brought home to him.

## Entered, Passed, Raised

The Candidate is, however, subjected to like personal experience in each of the Craft Degrees, and it calls to be understood thus. In the Entered Apprentice Degree it is because of a new life which he is to lead henceforth. In the Fellowcraft, it is as if the mind were to be renewed, for the prosecution of research in the hidden mysteries of nature, science, and art. But in the sublime Degree of Master Mason it is in order that he may enter fully into the mystery of death and of that which follows thereafter, being the great mystery of the Raising. The three technical and official words corresponding to the successive experiences are Entered, Passed, and Raised, their Craft-equivalents being Apprentice, Craftsman and Master—or he who has undertaken to acquire the symbolical and spiritualized art of building the house of another life; he who has passed therein to a certain point of proficiency, and in fine, he who has attained the whole mystery. If I may use for a moment the imagery of Francis Bacon, Lord Verulam, he has learned how to effectuate in his own personality 'a new birth in time', to wear a new body of desire, intention and purpose; he has fitted to that body a new mind, and other objects of research. In fine, he has been taught how to lay it aside, and yet again he has been taught how to take it up after a different manner, in the midst of a very strange symbolism.

## Imperfect Symbolism

Now, it may be observed that in delineating these intimations of our symbolism, I seem already to have departed from the mystery of building with which I opened the conference; but I have been actually considering various sidelights thereon. It may be understood, further, that I am not claiming to deal with a symbolism that is perfect in all its parts, however honourable it may be otherwise to the builder. In the course of such researches as I have been enabled to make into the Instituted Mysteries of different ages and countries, I have never met with one which was in entire harmony with itself. We must be content with what we have, just as it is necessary to tolerate the peculiar conventions of language under which the Craft Degrees have passed into expression, artificial and sometimes commonplace as they are. Will you observe once again at this stage how it is only in the first Degree that the Candidate is instructed to build upon his own part a superstructure which is somehow himself? This symbolism is lost completely in the ceremony of the Fellowcraft Degree, which, roughly speaking, is something of a Degree of Life; the symbols being more especially those of conduct and purpose, while in the Third Degree, they speak of direct relations between man and his Creator, giving intimation of judgment to come.

## The Third Degree

I have said, and you know, that the Master Degree is one of death and resurrection of a certain kind, and among its remarkable characteristics there is a return to building symbolism, but this time in the form of a legend. It is no longer an erection of the Candidate's own house—house of the body, house of the mind, and house of the moral law. We are taken to the Temple of Solomon and are told how the Master-Builder suffered martyrdom rather than betray the mysteries which had been placed in his keeping. Manifestly the lesson which is drawn in the Degree is a veil of something much deeper, and about which there is no real intimation. It is assuredly an instruction for the Candidates that they must keep the secrets of the Masonic Order secretly, but such a covenant has reference only to the official and external side. The bare recitation of the legend would have been sufficient to enforce this; but observe that the Candidate assumes the part of the Master-Builder and suffers within or in him—as a testimony of personal faith and honour in respect to his own engagements. But thereafter he rises, and it is this which gives a peculiar characteristic to the descriptive title of the Degree. It is one of raising and of reunion with companions—almost as if he had been released from earthly life and had entered into the true Land of the Living. The keynote is therefore not one of dying but one of resurrection; and yet it is not said in the legend that the Master rose. The point seems to me one of considerable importance, and yet I know not of a single place in our literature wherein it has received consideration. I will leave it, however, for the moment, but with the intention of returning to it.

## Part II

There are two ways in which the Master Degree may be thought to lapse from perfection in respect of its symbolism, and I have not taken out a licence to represent it as of absolute order in these or in any respects. This has been practically intimated already. Perhaps it is by the necessity of things that it has recourse always to the lesser meaning, for it is this which is more readily understood. On the other hand, much must be credited to its subtlety, here and there, in the best sense of the term. There is something to be said for an allegory which he who runs may read, at least up to a certain point. But those who made the legend and the ritual could not have been unaware of that which the deeper side shows forth; they have left us also the Opening and Closing as of the great of all greatness—so it seems to me, my Brethren—in things of ceremony and ritual. Both are devoid of explanation, and it is for us to understand them as we can.

For myself it is obvious that something distinct from the express motives of Masonry has come to us in this idea of Raising. The Instituted Mysteries of all ages and countries were concerned in the figuration, by means of ritual and symbolism, of New Birth, a new life, a mystic death and resurrection, as so many successive experiences through which the Candidate passed on the way of his inward progress from earthly to spiritual life, or from darkness to light. The Ritual or Book of the Dead is a case in point. It has been for a long period regarded by scholarship as intimating the after-death experiences or adventures of the soul in the halls of judgment, and so forth; but there are traces already of the genesis of a new view, chiefly in the writings of Mr W. Flinders Petrie, according to which some parts at least of this great text are really a rite of initiation and advancement, through which Candidates pass in this life.

## The Book of the Dead

If I am putting this rather strongly as regards one important authority, it is at least true to say that he appears to discern the mystical side of the old Egyptian texts, while there are others, less illustrious than he, who have gone much further in this direction. It is very difficult for one like myself, although unversed in Egyptology, to study such a work as 'Osiris and the Egyptian Resurrection', by E. Wallis Budge, without feeling very strongly that there is much to be said for this view, or without hoping that it will be carried further by those who are properly warranted.

So far as it is possible to speak of the Kabiric Mysteries, there was in those an episode of symbolical death, because Kasmillos, a technical name ascribed to the Candidate, was represented as slain by the gods. Some of the rites which prevailed within and around Greece in ancient times are concerned with the idea of a regeneration or new birth. The Mysteries of Bacchus depicted the death of this god and his restoration to light as Rhea. Osiris died and rose, and so also did Adonis. He was first lamented as dead and then his revivification was celebrated with great joy. There is no need, however, to multiply the recurrence of these events in the old Mysteries nor to restrict ourselves within their limits, for all religions have testified to the necessity of regeneration and have administered its imputed processes. That which is most important—from my point of view—is the testimony belonging to Christian times and the secret tradition therein.

## The Christian Mysteries

Of course, to speak of this it is necessary to tread on subjects which at the present are excluded, and very properly so, from discussion in a Craft Lodge, when they are presented from a religious and doctrinal angle. I shall not treat them from that standpoint, but rather as a sequence of symbolism in the form of dramatic mystery, alluding slightly, and from a philosophical point of view only, to the fact that in certain schools they are regarded as delineating momentous experiences in the history and life of man's soul. That new birth which conferred upon the Eleusinian mystae the title of Regenerated Children of the Moon—so that each one of them was henceforth symbolically a Son of the Queen of Heaven—born as a man originally and reborn in a divine manner—has its correspondence on a much higher plane of symbolism with the Divine Birth in Bethlehem, according to which a child was 'born' and a son 'given', who, in hypothesis at least, was the Son of God, but Son also of Mary—one of whose titles, according to Latin theology, is Queen of Heaven.

The hidden life in Egypt and Nazareth corresponds to the life of seclusion led by the mystae during their period of probation between the Lesser and Great Mysteries. The three years of ministry are in analogy with the Temple-functions of the mystagogues. But lastly, in Egypt and elsewhere, there was the mystic experience of the Pastos, in which the initiate dies symbolically, as Jesus died upon the Cross. The Christian 'Symbolum' says:—*Descendit ad inferos*: that is, 'He descended into hell'; and in the entranced condition of the Pastos, the soul of the Postulant was held or was caused to wander in certain spiritual realms. But in fine, it is said of Christ:—*Tertia die resurrexit*: 'the third day he rose again from the dead'. So also the Adept of the Greater Mysteries rose from the Pastos in the imputed glory of an inward illumination.

## The Mystical Fact

There was a period not so long ago when these analogies were recognized and applied to place a fabulous construction upon the central doctrines of Christian religion, just as there was a period when the solar mythology was adapted in the same direction. We have no call to consider these aberrations of a partially digested learning; but they had their excuses in their period. The point on which I would insist is that in the symbolism of the old initiations, and in the pageant of the Christian mythos, there is held to be the accurate delineation of a mystical experience, the head and sections of which correspond to the notions of mystic birth, life, death and resurrection. It is a particular formula which is illustrated frequently in the mystic literature of the western world. Long before symbolical Masonry had emerged above the horizon, several cryptic texts of alchemy, in my understanding, were bearing witness to this symbolism and to something real in experience which lay behind it. In more formal Christian mysticism, it was not until the sixteenth century and later that it entered into the fullest expression.

Now, that which is formulated as mystic birth is comparable to a dawn of spiritual consciousness. It is the turning of the whole life-motive in the divine direction, so that, at a given time—which is actually the point of turning—the personality stands symbolically between the East and the North, between the greatest zone of darkness and that zone which is the source of light, looking towards the light-source and realizing that the whole nature has to be renewed therein. Mystic life is a quest of divine knowledge in a world that is within. It is the life led in this light, progressing and developing therein, as if a Brother should read the mysteries of Nature and Science with new eyes cast upon the record, which record is everywhere, but more especially in his own mind and heart. It is the complete surrender to the working of the divine, so that an hour comes when *proprium meum et tuum* dies in the mystical sense, because it is hidden in God. In this state, by the testimony of many literatures, there supervenes an experience which is described in a thousand ways yet remains ineffable. It has been enshrined in the imperishable books of Plato and Plotinus. It glimmers forth at every turn and corner of the remote roads and pathways of Eastern philosophies. It is in little books of unknown authorship, treasured in monasteries and most of which have not entered into knowledge, except within recent times.

## The Place of Darkness

The experience is in a place of darkness, where, in other symbolism, the sun is said to shine at midnight. There is afterwards that further state, in which the soul of man returns into the normal physical estate, bringing the knowledge of another world, the quest ended for the time being at least. This is compared to resurrection, because in the aftermath of his experience the man is, as it were, a new being. I have found in most mythological legends that the period between death and resurrection was triadic and is spoken of roughly as three days, though there is an exception in the case of Osiris, whose dismemberment necessitated a long quest before the most important of his organs was left finally lost. The three days are usually foreshortened at both ends; the first is an evening, the second a complete day, while the third ends at sunrise. It is an allusion to the temporal brevity ascribed in all literatures to the culminating mystical experience. It is remarkable, in this connection, that during the mystic death of the Candidate in the Third Degree, the time of his interned condition is marked by three episodes, which are so many attempts to raise him, the last only being successful.

## Operative Masonry

Two things follow unquestionably from these considerations, so far as they have proceeded. The interest in Operative Masonry and its records, though historically it is of course important, has proceeded from the beginning on a misconception as to the aims and symbolism of Speculative Masonry. It was and it remains natural, and it has not been without its results, but it is a confusion of the chief issues. It should be recognized henceforward that the sole connection between the two Arts and Crafts rests on the fact that the one has undertaken to uplift the other from the material plane to that of morals on the surface and of spirituality in the real intention. Many things led up thereto, and a few of them were at work unconsciously within the limits of Operative Masonry. At a period when there was a tendency to symbolize everything roughly, so that it might receive a tincture of religion—I speak of the Middle Ages—the duty of Apprentice to Master, and of Master to pupil, had analogies with relations subsisting between man and God, and they were not lost sight of in those old Operative documents. Here was a rudiment capable of indefinite extension. The placing of the Lodges and of the Craft at large under notable patronage, and the subsequent custom of admitting persons of influence, offered another and quite distinct opportunity. These facts notwithstanding, my position is that the traces of symbolism which may in a sense be inherent in Operative Masonry did not produce, by a natural develoment, the Speculative Art and Craft, though they helped undoubtedly to make a possible and partially prepared field for the great adventure and experiment.

## The Old Charges

The second point is that we must take the highest intention of symbolism in the Third Degree to some extent apart from the setting. You will know that the literary history of our ritual is rather non-existent than obscure, or if this is putting the case a little too strongly, it remains that researches have so far left the matter in a dubious position. The reason is not for our seeking, for the kind of enquiry that is involved is one of exceeding difficulty. If I may say that it is my personal aspiration to undertake it one of these days, I speak of what is perhaps a distant hope. That which is needed is a complete codification of all the old copies, in what language soever, which are scattered throughout the Lodges and libraries of the whole Masonic world, together with an approximate determination of their dates by expert evidence. In my opinion, the codices now in use have their roots in the eighteenth century. but were edited and re-edited at an even later date.

I have now brought before you in somewhat disjointed manner—as I cannot help feeling—several independent considerations, each of which, taken separately, institutes certain points of correspondence between Masonry and other systems of symbolism, but they do not at present enter into harmony. I will collect them as follows:-

(1) Masonry has for its object, under one aspect, the building of the Candidate as a house or temple of life. Degrees outside the Craft aspire to this building as a living stone in a spiritual temple, meet for God's service.

(2) Masonry presents also a symbolical sequence but in a somewhat crude manner, of Birth, Life, Death and Resurrection, which other systems indicate as a mystery of experience.

(3) Masonry, in fine, represents the whole body of its Adepti as in search of something that has been lost, and it tells us how and with whom that loss came about.

These are separate and independent lines of symbolism, though, as indicated already, they are interlinked by the fact of their incorporation in Craft Masonry, considered as a unified system. But the truth is that between the spiritual building of the First Degree and the Legend of Solomon's Temple there is so little essential correspondence that the one was never intended to lead up to the other. The symbolism of the Entered Apprentice Degree is of the simplest and most obvious kind; it is also personal and individualistic. That of the Master Degree is complex and remote in its significance; it is, moreover, an universal mythos. I have met with some searchers of the mysteries who seem prepared to call it cosmic, but I must not carry you so far as this speculation would lead us, and I do not hold a brief for its defence. I am satisfied in my own mind that the Third Degree has been grafted on the others and does not belong to them. There has been no real attempt to weld them, but they have been drawn into some kind of working sequence by the Exhortation which the Worshipful Master recites prior to the dramatic scene in the last Master Degree. To these must be added some remarks to the Candidate immediately after the Raising. The Legend is reduced therein to the uttermost extent possible in respect of its meaning, though it is possible that this has been done of set purpose.

## Living Stones

It will be seen that the three aspects enumerated above fall under two heads in their final analysis, the first representing a series of practical counsels, thinly allegorized upon in terms of symbolical architecture. The Candidate is instructed to work towards his own perfection under the light of Masonry. There is no mystery, no concealment whatever, and it calls for no research in respect of its source. Its analogies and replicas are everywhere, more especially in religious systems. It is a reflection of the Pauline doctrine that man is or may become a temple of the Holy Spirit. But it should be observed in this connection that there is a rather important though confusing mixture of images in the address of the Worshipful Master to the Candidate, after the latter has been invested and brought to the East. It is pointed out to him that he represents the cornerstone of a building—as it might be, the whole Masonic edifice—but he is immediately counselled to raise a superstructure from the foundation of that corner-stone—thus reversing the image. That of the corner-stone is like an externalization in dramatic form of an old Rosicrucian maxim belonging to the year 1620:—'Be ye transmuted from dead stones into living, philosophical stones'.

From my point of view, it is the more important side of the symbolism; it is as if the great Masonic edifice were to be raised on each Candidate; and if every Neophyte shaped his future course both in and out of Masonry, as though this were the case actually, I feel that the Royal Art would be other than it now is and that our individual lives would differ.

### PART III

Recurring to the Legend of the Third Degree, the pivot upon which it revolves is the existence of a building secret, represented as a Master-Word, which the Builder died to preserve. Owing to his untimely death, the Word was lost, and it has always been recognized in Masonry that the Temple, unfinished at the moment of the untoward event, remained with its operations suspended and was completed later on by those who obviously did not possess the Word or key. The tradition has descended to us and, as I have said, we are still on the quest.

Now what does this all mean? We have no concern at the present day, except in archaeology and history with King Solomon's Temple. What is meant by this Temple and what is the Lost Word? These things have a meaning, or our system is stultified. Well, here are burning questions, and the only direction in which we can look for an answer is that which is their source. As to this, we must remember that the Legend of the Master Degree is a Legend of Israel, under the aegis of the Old Covenant, and though it has no warrants in the Holy Writ which constitutes the Old Testament, it is not antecedently improbable that something to our purpose may be found elsewhere in the literature of Jewry.

## The Kabalah

I do not of course mean that we shall meet with the Legend itself; it would be interesting if we did but not *per se* helpful, apart from explanation. I believe in my heart that I have found what is much more important, and this is the root-matter of that which is shadowed forth in the Legend, as regards the meaning of the Temple and the search for the Lost Word. There are certain great texts which are known to scholars under the generic name of Kabalah, a Hebrew word meaning reception, or doctrinal teaching passed on from one to another by verbal communication. According to its own hypothesis, it entered into written records during the Christian era, but hostile criticism has been disposed to represent it as invented at the period when it was written. The question does not signify for our purpose, as the closing of the thirteenth century is the latest date that the most drastic view—now generally abandoned—has proposed for the most important text.

We find therein after what manner, according to mystic Israel, Solomon's Temple was spiritualized; we find deep meaning attached to the two pillars J. and B.; we find how the word was lost and under what circumstances the chosen people were to look for its recovery. It is an expectation for Jewish theosophy, as it is for the Craft Mason. It was lost owing to an untoward event, and although the time and circumstances of its recovery have been calculated in certains texts of the Kabalah, there has been something wrong with the methods. The keepers of the tradition died with their faces toward Jerusalem, looking for that time; but for Jewry at large the quest is continued by us in virtue of a ceremonial formula but cannot be said to mean anything for those who undertake and pursue it. It was lost owing to the unworthiness of Israel, and the destruction of the First Temple was one consequence thereof. By the waters of Babylon, in their exile, the Jews are said to have remembered Zion, but the word did not come back into their hearts; and when Divine Providence inspired Cyrus to bring about the building of the Second Temple and the return of Israel into their own land, they went back empty of all recollection in this respect.

## The Divine Name

I am putting things in a summary fashion that are scattered up and down the vast text with which I am dealing—that is to say, *Sepher Ha Zohar*, the Book of Splendour. The word to which reference is made is the Divine Name out of the consonants of which, *He, Vau, He, Yod*, we have formed Jehovah, or more accurately Yahve. When Israel fell into a state which is termed impenitence it is said in the Zoharic Symbolism that the *Vau* and the *He* final were separated. The name was dismembered, and this is the first sense of loss which is registered concerning it. The second is that it has no proper vowel points, those of the Name *Elohim* being substituted, or alternatively the Name Adonai. It is said, for example: 'My Name is written *YHVH* and read Adonai'. The epoch of restoration and completion is called, almost indifferently, that of resurrection, the world to come, and the advent of the Messiah. In such a day the present imperfect separation between the letters will be put an end to, once and forever. If it be asked: What is the connection between the loss and dismemberment which befell the Divine Name Jehovah and the Lost Word in Masonry, I cannot answer too plainly; but every Royal Arch Mason knows that which is communicated to him in that Supreme Degree, and in the light of the present explanation he will see that the 'great' and 'incomprehensible' thing so imparted comes to him from the Secret Tradition of Israel.

It is also to this Kabalistic source, rather than to the variant accounts in the first book of Kings and in Chronicles, that we must have recourse for the important Masonic Symbolism concerning the Pillars J. and B. There is very little in Holy Scripture which would justify a choice of these objects as particular representatives of our art of building spiritualized. But in later Kabalism, in the texts called *The Garden of Pomegragates* and in *The Gates of Light*, there is a very full and complicated explanation of the strength which is attributed to B., the left-hand Pillar, and of that which is established in and by the right-hand Pillar, called J.

## The Temple

As regards the Temple itself, I have explained at length elsewhere after what manner it is spiritualized in various Kabalistic and semi-Kabalistic texts, so that it appears ever as 'the proportion of the height, the proportion of the depth, and the lateral proportions' of the created universe, and again as a part of the transcendental mystery of law which is at the root of the secret tradition in Israel. This is outside our subject, not indeed by its nature but owing to limitations of opportunity. I will say only that it offers another aspect of a fatal loss in Israel and the world—which is commented on in the tradition. That which the Temple symbolized above all things was, however, a House of Doctrine, and as on the one hand the Zohar shows us how a loss and substitution were perpetuated through centuries, owing to the idolatry of Israel at the foot of Mount Horeb in the wilderness of Sinai, and illustrated by the breaking of the Tables of Stone on which the Law was inscribed; so does Speculative Masonry intimate that the Holy House, which was planned and begun after one manner, was completed after another and a word of death was substituted for a word of life.

## The Builder

I shall not need to tell you that beneath such veils of allegory and amidst such illustrations of symbolism, the Master-Builder signifies a principle and not a person, historical or otherwise. He signifies indeed more than a single principle, for in the world of mystic intimations through which we are now moving, the question, 'Who is the Master?' would be answered by many voices. But generically, he is the imputed life of the Secret-Doctrine which lay beyond the letter of the Written Law, which 'the stiff-necked and disobedient' of the patriarchal, sacerdotal and prophetical dispensations contrived to destroy. According to the Secret Tradition of Israel, the whole creation was established for the manifestation of this life, which became manifested actually in its dual aspect when the spiritual Eve was drawn from the side of the spiritual Adam and placed over against him, in the condition of face to face. The intent of creation was made void in the event which is called the Fall of Man, though the particular expression is unknown in Scripture. By the hypothesis, the 'fatal consequences' which followed would have reached their time on Mount Sinai, but the Israelites, when left to themselves in the wilderness, 'sat down to eat and rose up to play'. That which is concealed in the evasion of the last words corresponds to the state of Eve in Paradise, when she had become infected by the serpent.

To sum up as regards the sources, the Lost Word in Masonry is derived from a Kabalistic thesis of imperfection in the Divine Name Jehovah, by which the true pronunciation—that is to say, the true meaning—is lost. It was the life of the House of Doctrine, represented by the Temple planned of old in Israel. The Master-Builder is the Spirit, Secret or Life of the Doctrine; and it is the quest of this that every Mason takes upon himself in the ceremony of the Third Degree, so that the House, which in the words of another Masonic Degree, is now, for want of territory, built only in the heart, 'a superstructure perfect in its parts and honourable to the builder'.

## Craft Masonry

But if these are the sources of Craft Masonry, taken at its culmination in the Sublime Degree, what manner of people were those who grafted so strange a speculation and symbolism on the Operative procedure of a building-Guild? The answer is that all about that period which represents what is called the transition, or during the sixteenth and seventeenth centuries, the Latin-writing scholars were animated with zeal for the exposition of the tradition in Israel, with the result that many memorable and even great books were produced on the subject. Among those scholars were many great names, and they provided the materials ready to the hands of the symbolists. What purpose had the latter in view? The answer is that in Germany, Italy, France and England, the zeal for Kabalistic literature among the Latin-writing scholars had not merely a scholastic basis. They believed that the texts of the Secret Tradition showed plainly, out of the mouth of Israel itself, that the Messiah had come. This is the first fact. The second I have mentioned already, namely that although the central event of the Third Degree is the Candidate's Raising, it is not said in the Legend that the Master-Builder rose, thus suggesting that something remains to come after, which might at once complete the Legend and conclude the quest. The third fact is that in a rather early and important High Degree of the philosophical kind, now almost unknown, the Master-Builder of the Third Degree rises as Christ, and so completes the dismembered Divine Name, by insertion of the Hebrew letter Shin, this producing *Yehoshua*—the restoration of the Lost Word in the Christian Degrees of Masonry.

Of course, I am putting this point only as a question of fact in the development of symbolism. Meanwhile, I trust that, amidst many imperfections, I have done something to indicate a new ground for our consideration, and to show that the speaking mystery of the Opening and Closing of the Third Degree and the Legend of the Master-Builder come from what may seem to us very far away, but yet not so distant that it is impossible to trace them to their source.

# 11
# THE VEIL OF THE SANCTUM SANCTORUM

Freemasonry was for Waite only one of the many paths of the Secret Tradition, but it was yet among the most important, and one of his constant cares was to emphasize the correspondence he saw between mysticism and masonry. In 1906 he included in his book *Studies in Mysticism* a series of papers dedicated to that end. All of them had been published earlier in *Horlick's Magazine* (which Waite edited), but only the final paper, *The Innermost Sanctuary*, was altered to any extent. Waite had been dissatisfied with the text and, feeling that revision was impossible, he rewrote it as *The Veil of the Sanctum Sanctorum*. It is this delightful, wholly transformed version that is printed here.

I HAVE said something in previous papers concerning the historical side of Masonry in its correspondence with other mysteries, and seeing that in most cases the available facts, or those things for which there is evidence in documents, are rather concerned with the *minima*, I have leaned naturally towards the high speculations, if I may so term them—towards those grades and orders which are held usually to stand apart from the authentic and recognized concerns of Masonry, embodying in some respects matters which were of faith among particular brethren in the past, and at most—but this in rare instances—representing certain derivations from a comparative antiquity, for which, however, the evidence—outside the testimony of the rite—is not to be found in documents. That is to say, they are voices speaking almost behind the veil, and this scarcely otherwise than in the sense of oracles. It is not only through these that Masonry connects with the great past of the mysteries, and indeed the root legends speak with a clear tone, though it is not exactly in a language which is understood by the initiates at large, nor is the bond of consanguinity of that kind which is so unmistakable that none can fail in its recognition. There is, however, one form of sacramentalism which characterizes all the orders of initiation, and is found, at least as an implicit, in all grades. It is that which is usually missed, because it is so easy to miss the great things that are not in patent evidence and are not, so to speak, written in the starry heavens. This mystery has already been enunciated in the simple statment that all initiation is concerned with communicating, by the office of symbols, a new life, which is depicted most commonly as a Mystery of Inward Generation. It proclaims, in other words, to every candidate, that 'except a man be born again' he shall not enter—that is, essentially and truly—into the Secret Kingdom of the Rites. There are certainly many lesser orders, assemblies and confraternities which, having little or no inheritance from the past, offer scarcely any trace of that sacramental life which is understood in the idea of rebirth; but the implication to which I have referred is found under very curious conditions, and I am not sure that among all the places of seclusion there is one place where we shall fail to discern it enshrined, though it lies sometimes far below the common plummet of the interpretation of symbols. It is not by this alone, but it is at least by this above all, that all are inter-connected, as by one root belonging to a great tree of concealed life and brotherhood. It is this which makes the mystery of redemption in Christ a great mystery of initiation and advancement; it is this which makes Masonry a mirror not only of all the instituted mysteries which went before it, but of many which have subsisted concurrently, and also the elder sister of some which are still among us, less obvious than she is, but less unconscious on the surface of their proper geniture and pedigree. It is, therefore, in the reconsideration of this doctrine, however indirectly and under all reserves whatsoever, that the last message of these papers on the higher sense of brotherhood can be most simply put forth. It is not by any means essential that we should speak of Masonry apart from, or in preference to, organisms by which it is encircled and into which it is unofficially incorporated; but standing as the pattern for many, it testifies for others besides itself and can be held for the present purpose to include them.

If it were possible to take unexpectedly a census of opinion within the ranks of the Masonic Fraternity on the general subject of rites, and on the place of Masonry among them, I suppose that such opinion, missing the real point at issue, would fall unconventionally into two groups, plus a residuum which numerically would be almost negligible and one which, for the purpose of this brief study, can also be set aside at the moment. The two groups would consist, on the one hand, of those who regard Masonry as complete in the craft degrees, which might or might not include the Holy Royal Arch. The contrasted section would be much more composite in its character, but its members would be in agreement at least upon one point, and that point the antithesis of the preceding opinion, maintaining, as it is compelled in order to justify its own titles, that the Masonic experiment must be taken further than the admitted limits of the craft before it can be brought to perfection. The issue is in each instance so keen and clear that no intermediate ground or place of adjustment seems possible. There is no intention here of adjudicating upon either view, and they are cited only to put on record that the rites of initiation for the ordinary member of the craft would be really but one rite divided into three degrees, beyond which lies the vast region of fantasy. On the other hand, the advocates of the high grades would multiply them almost indefinitely, according to their particular system, but for these as for those the ideas of initiation and advancement would still lie within the circle, narrow or expanded, of that which they regard as Masonry.

The horizon, then, is to this extent restricted, because the question of the place of Masonry itself among rites understood generically,—supposing, as we must suppose, by the hypothesis of our own speculation, that there are mysteries of initiation and advancement which are outside the bonds of the Fraternity, however extensible,—may be well enough calculated to raise in most minds only a vague wonder. The inevitable inquiry will be: What rites? and behind them, what mysteries? Those who ask it may remember perhaps the ceremonial forms which serve the purposes of external and official religion. They may anticipate that the subsurface intention is to connect masonry, since it is from the standpoint of this one order that they can alone approach the question, with some system of doctrinal belief. As to this, they will know, or probably, that several authorities in the craft have been disposed to regard Masonic principles as equivalent in their application to such a hallowing of conduct and life as we attribute to religious processes. But there are others, and those indeed whose views are accepted more generally, for whom the basis of Masonry consists, like that of some other systems, wholly in moral conduct, founded, it is true, upon certain doctrines which are the heart and marrow of religion, but raised in their superstructure with sufficient independence to make two fabrics and two institutions, necessarily in harmony, necessarily working together, and yet logically distinct.

There is again no occasion to offer any judgment, however conditional; for no analogy of external religion enters into the present subject; and once more it is mentioned only to liberate the ground from a very natural misapprehension. The questions therefore recur: To what sequence of Rites, accepting the standpoint of the brethren, can Masonry be regarded as belonging? And what Mysteries does the suggestion suppose to underlie all? There are some orders and societies within the ranks of the great order which exist for studies that are designed to reply to these questions, and one can therefore, by the hypothesis at least, address the members of these with a reasonable certainty of being understood, and, if not commanding agreement, may in any case enlist sympathy. Still it is easy, indeed too easy, to overstep the field which is common to interested students who have proceeded a certain distance, and to enter in those regions of specialism and technicality the proper language of which sounds foreign to unaccustomed ears. I would therefore, in the first place, invite the clemency of Masonic, and generally of initiated people, if for those who know more I enumerate things familiar as if they were in a manner abstruse, and if for those who know less I should appear occasionally to exceed the normal measures of apprehension. The gift of speaking or writing in unknown tongues used to be regarded as exceptional, but it seems rather common with the specialist, and he has a luckless habit of lapsing into it unawares. The way of utterance on these subjects in the open face of day is eminently a way of prudence, but, maintaining all reserves, it is still possible, in a general manner, to say something of the Masonic experiment, assuming and not conveying the particular kind of knowledge in which the essence of the Fraternity is enshrined. In the light of the experience which all brethren of all initiations, within and without Masonry, have brought away from all degrees whatsoever, I must ask them then to consider for a moment the idea of rebirth. That is a tradition or a doctrine which may assuredly seem at first to lie apart from the field of the subject, yet it should be known in the connection which I have established under other forms of symbolism, and there is no call that I should put it more clearly. It will be known also by every one, independently of all associations except the great sodality of Christendom, that a most available source of information, and one who is more than a master, has told us that we do not put into the earth that which will come forth out of the earth, but that we sow something which is natural, to reap in due season what is spiritual. It follows also from St Paul that we sow what is dead, but that we look for something which is alive and will indeed live for ever. Now certain schools of symbolism and several secret orders teach, and have long taught, that some sacred and highly symbolic object, which varies in each Fraternity, once entered into the region of death, with sacramental accessories in the legend of certain rites, whereby the conditions of death and even of disintegration are made indubitable; but that something also issues forth and is found to be alive. It is not exactly the same, for even in the symbolic order a substitution has occurred, and this is really a vital point of the mystery. It may be said, if we prefer, that the mystical remanents of a sacred and solemn object are put into the seclusion and the darkness, and that which is brought forth is the vessel of the reception, which is true according to the symbolism; but the intention of the picture is really more exalted and secret. We should preferably consider that what is remitted into the region of the shadow is more properly the vessel of the reception, and that what comes forth is the sacred object, Let it be remembered that in the great sacramentalisms of Christian doctrine, a place of rest was prepared for One who was a man of sorrows and acquainted with infirmity, after the payment of the last farthing exacted by his enemies, while that which was manifested again upon the third day was manifested as the Lord of Glory. There are certain secret orders on the continent of Europe which in spite of their comparative antiquity and great historical import-ance, are unknown, even by name, in England, but in which this mystery is actually represented to the candidate as the final evolution of one important legend. Speaking as a student who, under this or another obedience, holds nearly all the existing rites, I can say, with first-hand knowledge, that, clouded by many veils and under the elusive appearance of almost numberless aspects, the same symbolical intention recurs continually. It does not in respect of the craft, so far as this is concerned in the present thesis, exactly complete the craft, since that, if exhaustively considered, will be found to contain the whole subject, but it interprets it after various manners and often illuminates it newly. It is just perhaps to add, since it will make for historical precision in these abstruse matters, that not only in certain cases is the veiling exceedingly thick, but even the method of expression and the particular materials of the symbolism would suggest that the operation of the conception has been implied rather than patent in the consciousness of some makers of rituals. In other words, they did not quite realize the full significance of that which they were moved to set forth, an experience well known to Saint-Martin, one of the greatest of the French mystics, himself also a Mason, and accredited, correctly or not, with the reconstitution of several grades and orders belonging to his period.

Having attempted to treat the general symbolism of the mysteries, both here and previously, from the standpoint of the idea of rebirth, the next question for consideration is the particular significance which should be attached to this idea so far as modern Fraternities are concerned. In this connection the analogies which I have been led to create with the central mysteries of Christendom, and the interpretation placed on one doctrine by the authority of St Paul, will naturally suggest that I regard it from what must necessarily be termed a religious standpoint. It would seem, therefore, and this almost indubitably, that I am renouncing categorically the course which I took at the beginning, and am pledging myself to the opinion that after all Masonry, if we must speak more especially of this one Brotherhood, is a matter of religious belief or knowledge rather than a manner of conduct. It is necessary however to distinguish, as happens so invariably in cases of this kind, between questions of instruction, the morality of grades and liturgies, and the content of symbolism. It is impossible, and indeed superfluous, to recite the instructions which are given to candidates at the various stages of their progess through any of the secret orders, or the duties which are definitely imposed on them and with which the least among the members of each sodality will be so entirely familiar. This body of teaching is one thing, and the fact that it is exceedingly valuable is further exhibited by another fact with which also we are unfortunately familiar in all our daily life. I mean to say that if the world at large, or even the mystic world, were guided by the principles of conduct inculcated in the ranks of any one of the Fraternities, the general trend of human history would be almost radically different from anything which it now is. The symbolism of the orders calls for, however, and will repay consideration, apart from any instituted system of moral teaching, which, vital as it is otherwise in its character, contains nothing of the nature of a mystery; and we have seen, I think, quite clearly that by the essence of things there can be nothing which is secret or peculiar about it. The concealed part of Masonry, for example, may of course be regarded as consisting in the fact of its externals, in the methods of communication by which Masons are accustomed to recognize each other, and so forth; but these at most are only the accidents and conventions, and it is an open knowledge with every one that in many cases, they have been betrayed times out of number. The true secret is concerned entirely with the symbolism, and this is why one school of interpretation has in the past gone so far as to say, and not without justification, that the mysteries are not taught openly even in the orders themselves. What happens actually is that certain keys are put into the hands of the brethren, as each initiate in his turn passes through the successive grades; and it is for him, if he is able, to open the Temple into which they may or do give entrance. Perhaps this is equivalent to saying that there may be good brethren innumerable in the craft and the other orders for whom the higher significance of their mystery has, by the constitution of their minds, remained almost sealed; but in any case the assumption that the symbolism is really concerned with subjects which are of the first importance, and indeed of the only importance to humanity, understood both within and without the fleeting experience of an earthly life, will inevitably mean that it must connect with religion, since religion is also concerned with the same subject. I suppose it may be taken for granted that there are many good men in the world for whom the conception of an immortal life and whatsoever is implied in the idea of a resurrection from the dead, together with that of a Personal

Deity, have ceased practically to be any motive of conduct. Now, as a working system of ethics independently of these doctrines seems entirely possible, it would follow that if Masonry, for example, consisted, as to its essence, wholly in the practice of charity among brethren, then a Fraternity without the Grand Architect of the Universe, and without any horizon opened out by the idea of another life, might well enough correspond to the lower notion of a Masonic brotherhood. The fact that these doctrines are an essential condition of membership is something more than a presumption that the essence of initiation is not contained within the limits of any principle of conduct, since ethics are not the *Summum Bonum*, not the totality of all forces at work in the development of man, nor actually the perfect way, though they are the gate of the way of perfection. It is further certain that the Biblical idea of resurrection, on which certain orders seem to lay stress exclusively, is only one aspect, and that accidental at best, of the conception of another life. The belief underlying these degrees would seem indubitably of the spiritual kind, and once transformed from the old tradition countenanced, under many reserves, by primeval Christianity, to the wider and deeper conception of the spiritual life, we may be led to conclude that, properly interpreted, the real doctrine current in the schools of initiation does not concern material resurrection, but rather spiritual rebirth. It is also in this way that it enters into that much wider sequence of rites the existence of which is suggested by the title of this essay. In respect of this there was a world before the modern schools, as there was a world before the Flood. I mean to say that the doctrines and the knowledge which are now enshrined in this or that order, as by a final transfiguration of symbols, were in older days contained, as we have seen, in certain mysteries of the past, some records of which have been happily preserved to us and can be disentangled, in spite of inherent imperfections and many corruptions. They appear then as now to be concerned always with the symbolism of mystic death, and in this connection I may mention that, almost as far back as human history goes in one particular direction, we find traces of rites worked in Samothrace, where the candidate was brought for the purposes of initiation into the presence of the gods, and was there slain by the gods. It will seem at first sight that this was a kind of mystery which even the enthusiastic disciple would have been disposed to avoid, at that as indeed at any other period; but, in the light of all which we know concerning the later orders, we shall of course interpret the episode wholly in a symbolical manner, and shall understand readily enough that the recipient was passing through an experience of symbolical death, subsequently to which he also experienced rebirth. The moving symbolism of Egyptian wisdom in 'The Book of the Dead', about which I am not in any sense competent to speak, operates in the same direction, for we know that at the end of the mysteries the dead also came forth alive. The records of Greek mysteries are equally express upon this subject as the symbolical term of initiation. We gather from many sources the importance which was always attached to them, and the wonderful illumination which, after some secret manner, was communicated, *ex hypothesi*, to the epopts.

Perhaps from one point of view the descent from the mysteries of Egypt into those of the classical world is like the descent of the soul into material things; but at least, according to the accepted tradition, Greece derived from Egypt, nor that at so great a distance, and carefully as its mysteries were concealed by those whom we believe to have passed through their chief grades, the fullest evidence remains in Plato, Plotinus, and others in the chain of philosophy, that such wisdom as inhered in the higher understanding of Greek mystic thought is identical as to its term with all that we can derive from ancient Egypt. I am writing of necessity as shortly as possible of these countries and periods to avoid undue repetition, and the subject-matter is scarcely within the horizon of conventional scholarship, which, in things Egyptian, is without any knowledge of symbols. Coming down to later times, and to the Christian dispensation, we find strange literatures which seem after their own manner to transmit from those who went before them a part of the same traditions, and to indicate concealed somewhere in the world the analogical aspects of identical knowledge. It is more than easy to err in investigations of this kind and to discern over-readily in mystic books something deeper than perhaps they were ever intended to convey. For example, there has been, both in this country and elsewhere, much idle speculation as to the real purpose behind such intellectual puzzles as the literature of Alchemy. Some exponents of this concealed art have been disposed to regard it as concerned exclusively with the experience of the soul in its progress, and have said that what took place in the alembics—themselves symbolic—of the philosophers was not the conversion of base metals and their reproduction in the perfect form of gold, but, on the contrary, that human nature was transmuted therein into a condition that, so far as its form permitted, became akin to divine nature. The lessons of the history and the fuller understanding of the literature are really in another direction, and there is no doubt at this day, among those most qualified to judge, that, at least in its primary aspects, Alchemy was a chemical experiment. It will be a matter of astonishment to most persons that there should be any need to establish a point which is to all appearances so obvious. The researches of M. Berthelot, who has published for the first time the *Byzantine Alchemists*, have read any alternative view a rather remarkable lesson, which so far none of his readers have appreciated. He has traced the undoubted metallic experiments of the Græco-Alexandrian period right through medieval times, and has created thereby at least one strong presumption as to the express objects of the art in connection with those great names which are familiar to the students of the subject. There will be no need to add that with any other point of view he, as a scientist, was quite naturally unacquainted. All this notwithstanding, the truth seems to lie rather in a middle ground, and the literature justifies us in regarding the experiment of Alchemy as to some extent twofold in its character; that is to say, in part it was a secret mystery of science, but in part also the symbolism of that science was pressed into the service of another order of experiment; and those who have regarded the soul, its phases and developments, as the particular object of research have not been far astray in respect of certain schools. The subject has, unfortunately, been too long in the hands of persons who understood neither material Alchemy nor the term of mystic thought, and it calls for adequate treatment under other auspices. Here I can only say that there came a time when the metallic experiments had fallen into great disrepute, and when there was in increasing predominance, by the evidence of the literature, of that transcendental object to which I have alluded. Writers like Khunrath seem to have concerned themselves wholly with the latter, and when Jacob Boehme came forward to interpret the Secret Mysteries of Religion, he used largely the terminology and the symbolism of Alchemy as his most ready method of expression. In this manner we are enabled to see that

Spiritual Alchemy was concerned, like the Ancient Mysteries and several later institutions, with the doctrine of rebirth; that is to say, with the passage of the soul from a sacramental death into a mystical life. The process has been familiar for centuries to many persons for whom all rites, mysteries, and concealed literatures of the past have been sealed things, for it is simply another phase of Christian teaching concerning the experience of conversion. We have, however, no occasion to dwell here on a matter which so particularly belongs to the churches and even to the sects, but it is well to register the fact, with the object of showing that, both within and without the circles of any secret knowledge, the same conceptions have so largely been present to the mind throughout many ages. Interpreting the term in its broadest sense, regeneration is the root and branch of all the instituted mysteries, and, however deeply implied, of Masonry in common with all. It has been said by one of the Masters that 'the divine spirit of a man is not one with his soul until after regeneration, which is the beginning of that intimate union which constitutes what is called mystically the marriage of the hierophant'; and, again, that when regeneration is fully attained, 'the divine spirit alone instructs the hierophant'.

So far as the past is concerned, incorporated mystic schools of the conscious order have scarcely existed in England, but there are traces of one sodality which connects with the present subject, and this is the Brotherhood of C.R.C., understood to be the initiates of the illuminated father, Christian Rosy Cross. if I may assume my readers' acquaintance with the German legend of the order, first made public in the earliest years of the seventeenth century, I would ask them to go back in mind for a few moments thereto; to remember how in his early years he went eastwards in search of wisdom; how he attained a certain proficiency in the mysteries which were treasured in the East; how he returned finally to Europe, bearing the records of his travels; and how he attempted a reformation of arts and sciences, with the result which, more especially at that period, attached to efforts of the kind. He was brought in the end to a resource which was not unusual among the custodians of secret knowledge; and the new birth of time, if I may borrow for a moment the phraseology of Francis Bacon, was committed to the custody of the secret society which he founded under the name of the Rosicrucians. The brethren of that order drifted apart from one another, and in due time it is said that there were later associates who did not appear to have received undoubted communication of the entire knowledge, and were even unacquainted with the actual resting-place of their founder when the hour came for him to pass from this life. Certain investigations which are described in the legend by the subterfuge of building operations results, however, in the discovery of the sepulchre which he had made, and there is a very full and significant account concerning it given in a manifesto of the Fraternity. It is, of course, a symbolical account, and its actual significance has received earnest consideration on the part of many students following different lines of research and producing as a consequence different results. However this may be, for the moment it serves our purpose to know that the tomb was opened, and among the many wonders which were discovered, an incidental reference informs us that the body of the Master was included, but in that condition which suggests that it was in some sense immortal and incorruptible. In other words, that which had been put under the altar had undergone the change of the altar. I do not know whether this point has so far been noticed either by occult students or by critics of the ordinary kind; but for my present purpose it is truly significant, because it indicates that, as in accordance with the idea of the old mysteries concerning rebirth and resurrection, something, as St Paul says, had been sown in the natural order, and something after some mysterious manner is represented as having been raised, as we would say, in the spiritual order. We might have expected to find that the tomb of Christian Rosy Cross was empty, like the tomb of Christ on Easter Day, but this would not accord with the symbolism, in which the idea of rebirth is veiled. It should be noted, however, that secret orders possessing an inheritance from the past, are now working the resurrection of C.R.C., as the final development of their rites, and for them at least, being dead, he yet speaketh.

I have devoted these few papers to Freemasonry in relation to universal initiation as a guide to those who are anxious to determine the kind of assistance which existing secret associations can give towards the elucidation of the old experiment of the mysteries. To exhaust the subject of the correspondences between Masonry and Mysticism would require many papers.

For these reasons and in this place I must leave it at the point that I have reached. Students who are sufficiently concerned may extend the researches which I can only pretend to have opened through further fields of analogy; they may institute a comparison between certain characteristics of Masonic liturgies and those of mystic literature; and they will find even in many titles of Masonic dignity an unintended reference to mysticism.

The world of symbolism is a world of many resurrections, and within their law and their order there is one among these which is not only of all the highest but the most symbolic of all. Though I have described Masonry as the mirror of instituted initiation, it has been with no idea of transcendence, to which it is indeed without a title. It is the most proximate and available of the illustrations, and its reflection is fairly complete, as of great things by little. In its development it has never succeeded in completing the house which it set out to build, and it is only as something very far away that it recalls—in part by antithesis—that which is the mystery of all in exaltation, the nearest indeed of all, but the least comprehended. I suppose it is unnecessary to say that I speak of the one Master who was neither Hiram nor another; those who enter into the comprehension of this mystery and, in fine, of all that which is veiled by the symbolic resurrection of the first Easter morning, will have no need of Masonry or the other instituted systems; and if ever what is known in the most secret of all sanctuaries could in any way be proclaimed on the housetops, their office would pass for ever, because, like the Lady of Shalott, in place of looking through the glass, and that inversely, we shall have looked to the mystic Camelot.

I have illustrated the weakness of the specialist by lapsing into abstruse matters and technicalities with the fatal facility of the just man when he falls seven times; but it is difficult to keep silence about the temple when the statues themselves speak. Let me therefore add, in conclusion, that if the doctrine of the New Birth is, as I understand it, the awakening from material life into that of the soul; if beyond the region of the senses there are houses not made with hands, where we shall be united in the holy assemblies to those who have elsewhere shared our exile; if therefore out of all this human darkness there come, in fine, light; and if this be also the testimony of religion, as it is certainly that of Masonry, then, as Martines de Pasqually said, we must even be content with what we have; and we may derive, in the last resource, a certain intellectual satisfaction that the higher knowledge of the Masonic Order does not differ generically from the higher understanding of the Faith, or either from that end which in all time has been the chief concern of man. The poets and their accomplished substitutes may please us, as they do indeed and certainly, but under all reserve I say that

*The proper study of mankind is God*

By such considerations as I have given to the existing rites and to that which they transmit from the past, we are led back to the one subject, as will be the postulant of the various orders who, having first conceived intellectually of the term of adeptship, goes in search of the light within them. He returns after long travelling, but he has described no barren circle of research, for to him will much have been communicated which otherwise he might never have attained, though it will not have been on subjects foreign to the implicits of his soul. This is equivalent to saying that the rites of initiation are certain formulæ of consciousness whereby that which is within him subsistently is educed; and as an offset to the common life of conventions this is in these days as much as can be reasonably expected from any office of the sanctuaries. It is possible that the postulant will be asked to try one journey more, but this time it will be in the region of first-hand experience, when he will realize how true is that dictum, already quoted from the old alchemists, that it is vain to attempt the practice till the working theory has been laid down. The possession of this he will owe to those things by which he has been so far guided. The path that, in this case, he will be called to follow henceforth, and possibly for ever, is that of the Holy Assembly, which I have named once in this book. It is not a path of grades and degrees by which the candidate is advanced symbolically to the heights. He will not enter any institution to whoch conventional recommendation is possible. The Assembly neither asks nor receives pledges, nor does it offer warrants or charters. It is perhaps, in so far as any designation is concerned, better spoken of under that title which I have named in another connection; silence in the mouth of the Almighty One. This is not because silence is imposed, but because entrance into the sodality is a certain matter of growth—a continual communication, as I have said, in the higher consciousness. The postulant for admission is such by the fact of his status. If the evidences of the Holy Assembly are so slight in mystic literature, although this is an intellectual difficulty, it must be remembered that we are dealing with a state which is in transcendence by comparison with all states manifested here below, being that, as I conceive it, in which the Subject is withdrawn no longer into secret places but into its own concealment. There is only one word more: Whether the postulant whom I have supposed succeeds or fails, he will learn that high reason warrants everything that has been said here to show that the mystic life leads no one from the life of the Church.

# INDEX OF PROPER NAMES

à Wood, A., 43
Adamson, H., 51
Anderson, J., 147
Andrea, J. V., 38
Ashmole, E., 35, 36, 39, 47, 49–60, 70, 141

Baader, F. von, 90n, 92n
Bacon, F. (Lord Verulam), 36, 141, 157, 181
Bacon, R., 48
Backhouse, W., 52, 53
Baldwin II, 103, 107
Barruel, A., 119
Baxter, Mrs L., 32
Beaujeu (nephew of De Molay), 110
Berthelot, M., 180
Brewer, H., 53
Budge, E. A. W., 160
Buhle, J. G., 34, 35
Burgo Nuovo, Archangelo de, 69

Cagliostro, 88
Cadet-Gassicourt, L., 119
Capnion (see Reuchlin, J.)
Carové, F. W., 21
Charles I (King of England), 150
Clavel, F. T. B., 120
Clement V (Pope), 103, 107, 118, 120

Collier, J., 53
Conder, R., 35n
Cooke, Matthew, 114
Craven, J. B., 57

d'Aumont, P., 101
De Quincey, T., 34
Dee, John, 141
Desaguliers, J. T., 33, 69, 70, 147
Dupuy, P., 99

Eirenaeus Philalethes, 47
Ellam, J., 53
Ellam, R., 53
Encausse, G., 87, 90n, 91, 92n, 93n, 118

Fenélon, F., 151
Findel, J. G., 139
Fludd, R., ch. 3 *passim*, 49, 57, 71, 105, 141
Fournié, Abbé, 93

Gassendi, P., 38
Gould, R. F., 35, 47, 51, 70, 139
Gurtler, N., 99

Heywood, T., 86
Hund, C. G., Baron von, 101, 102, 109, 118

James I, 105

Inman, T., 134

Karl von Hesse, Prince, 111
Khunrath, H., 48, 180
Kloss, G., 105, 119

Lefrance, 119
Liebistorf, Baron de, 91
Lully, R., 48

Maier, M., 36, 40, 43
Mainwaring, Col. H., 53
Marschall von Bieberstein, C. G., 101
Mersenne, M., 38
Mirandolo, Pico di, 69
Molay, J. de, 103, 107, 108, 110, 118, 121, 148, 150
Monjoie, 118
Moore, W. J. B. Macleod, 114

Newton, J. F., 13, 32, 153
Nicolai, F., 35, 51
Noffo Dei, 120

Orleans, P., Duc d', 118

Papus (*see* Encausse, G.)
Paracelsus, 112, 144
Payen, H. de, 104
Pasqually, M. de, 87, 88, 89, 90, 93, 94, 183
Penket, R., 53
Petrie, Sir W. M. F., 159
Petrus Puteamus, 99
Philippe le Bel, 103, 107, 118, 120
Pike, A., 49, 70, 112, 114, 116, 120, 121
Prichard, S., 79

Ragon, J. M., 34, 35, 52, 59, 112, 120, 142
Ramsay, A., Chevalier de, 99, 100, 101, 108, 111, 141, 151

Reghellini de Schio, M., 34, 119
Reuchlin, J., 69
Riccius, B., 69
Robespierre, F. J. M., 92
Rosenroth, Knorr von, 70

Saint-Martin, L. C. de, 87, 91
Schubart, J. C., 110
Scott, Leader (*see* Mrs Baxter)
Seton, A., 47
Starck, J. A. von, 111
Studion, S., 37, 41

Thory, C. A., 119

Vaughan, T., 47, 49, 54, 137
Voltaire, J. R. A. de, 99

Waite, A. E., 10–12, 13, 19, 31, 45, 73, 87, 97, 117, 123, 153, 171
  *Azoth*, 11
  *Brotherhood of the Rosy Cross*, 50
  *Emblematic Freemasonry*, 12, 19, 31
  *Esoteric History of Freemasonry*, 11
  *New Encyclopaedia of Freemasonry*, 12, 45, 117
  *Occult Sciences*, 11
  *Real History of the Rosicrucians*, 11
  *Secret Tradition in Freemasonry*, 10–11
  *Shadows of Life and Thought*, 11, 12
Werner, Z., 108, 110
Wilmshurst, W. L., 10
Willermoz, J. E., 89, 92
Wolfstieg, A., 105
Woodford, A. F. A., 101

Yarker, J., 10, 101

# Of further interest

# A. E. WAITE
## Magician of Many Parts
### Edited by R. A. Gilbert

Arthur Edward Waite (1857-1942) was unique: the first — and only — scholarly student of 'rejected knowledge' to emerge from the shadowy world of the Victorian occult revival. It was Waite who introduced Eliphas Lévi to the English-speaking world; Waite who made the classics of alchemical literature available in English; and it was Waite who, in 1903, recreated the Hermetic Order of the Golden Dawn from the ashes of its self-destruction.

But Waite was no mere occultist. He was also a poet who corresponded with Robert Browning and W. B. Yeats; a Bohemian who created dramatic rituals for Arthur Machen; and a mystic whose spiritual philosophy found noble expression in his Fellowship of the Rosy Cross — the esoteric Order that so profoundly influenced Charles Williams. Besides these, and other, spheres of influence, all modern occult iconography is indebted to Waite for the Tarot pack, executed by the artist Pamela Colman Smith, that bears his name and that was used by T. S. Eliot as the symbolic structure of *The Waste Land*.

In this, the first biography of Waite, R. A. Gilbert has drawn on an extensive range of published and unpublished sources, as well as on his own unrivalled knowledge of Waite's *milieu*, to present an engaging and accurate portrait of a truly remarkable man.

# THE GOLDEN DAWN COMPANION

## A Guide to the History, Structure and Workings of the Hermetic Order of the Golden Dawn

### Compiled and Introduced by R. A. Gilbert

The Hermetic Order of the Golden Dawn epitomized the paradox of an intellectual élite who rejected orthodox religion and yet remained within the social establishment of its day. The colourful story of these would-be magicians is well known to students of nineteenth-century social history, but the private archives on which the definitive history of the Order (Ellic Howe's *The Magicians of the Golden Dawn*) was based have remained inaccessible to scholars.

But now this material has been made available for study and the texts of both official and unofficial documents can at last be published. Here are the full texts of the Order's Constitution, Rules and Regulations, the Obligations of candidates for both the Outer and Inner Orders, the 'General Orders' of the R.R. et A.C., and the complete membership list from the official Address Book, together with detailed descriptions of the Temples, the Grade rituals, and the manuscripts that comprise the archives.

In addition, the original texts of the various theories of origin of the Golden Dawn are brought together for the first time, and there is a comprehensive bibliography of all printed material relating to the Order.

# THE MAGICIANS OF THE GOLDEN DAWN

A Documentary History of a Magical Order
1887-1923

By Ellic Howe

The Hermetic Order of the Golden Dawn was launched upon an unsuspecting world in 1888, since when it has become the linchpin of modern occultism. It still has its enthusiastic adherents.

But the Golden Dawn was much more than a late-Victorian magical sodality. It was a social phenomenon, attracting poets, artists, writers, gentlemen scholars, even a Church of England clergyman (the Revd W. A. Ayton), as well as Rosicrucians, Freemasons, Theosophists, and occultists of all persuasions.

Ellic Howe's scholarly and entertaining study has established itself as the definitive account of the Golden Dawn. Based on a formidable array of hitherto inaccessible sources, it remains the most detailed account of the Order's tangled and stormy history from its inception in 1887 to 1923.

W. Wynn Westcott, S. L. Macgregor Mathers, Aleister Crowley, W. B. Yeats, A. E. Waite, Dion Fortune, and Arthur Machen were all associated with the Golden Dawn or its offshoots, besides many other, now largely forgotten, aspirants to occult knowledge. In many ways, as Ellic Howe remarks, it is a 'mad chronicle', but it is also a story with considerable historical and human interests. *The Magicians of the Golden Dawn* will delight all lovers of the bizarre, and accurately inform all those who wish to know the true history of the greatest occult society of them all.

# HERMETIC PAPERS OF A. E. WAITE

The Unknown Writings of a Modern Mystic

Edited by R. A. Gilbert

Arthur Edward Waite stands alone among the major figures of the 'Occult Revival'. He recognized both the requirements of scholarship and the practical needs of the aspiring mystic, and in his published works achieved a rare balance between the two. Yet much of his work remains unknown, for many of his essays were prepared exclusively for members of his esoteric Order — the Independent and Rectified Rite of the Golden Dawn — and have never appeared in print.

Now, in this major anthology of Waite's unknown writings, the most significant of these papers are published for the first time. They include essays and studies on the Hermetic Tradition that have long been virtually impossible to obtain: papers that Waite published privately or produced for obscure and now forgotten journals. Here are remarkable essays on the English Rosicrucians, on Kabbalistic Alchemy, and on 'The Tarot and the Rosy Cross', as well as other rarities of hermetic literature.